Walter Benjamin

The Work of Art in the Age of Mechanical Reproduction

TRANSLATED BY J. A. UNDERWOOD

PENGUIN BOOKS — GREAT IDEAS

PENGUIN BOOKS

Published by the Penguin Group
Penguin Books Ltd, 80 Strand, London WC2R 0RL, England
Penguin Group (USA) Inc., 375 Hudson Street, New York, New York 10014, USA
Penguin Group (Canada), 90 Eglinton Avenue East, Suite 700, Toronto, Ontario, Canada M4P 2Y3
(a division of Pearson Penguin Canada Inc.)
Penguin Ireland, 25 St Stephen's Green, Dublin 2, Ireland
(a division of Penguin Books Ltd)
Penguin Group (Australia), 250 Camberwell Road, Camberwell, Victoria 3124, Australia
(a division of Pearson Australia Group Pty Ltd)
Penguin Books India Pvt Ltd, 11 Community Centre, Panchsheel Park, New Delhi – 110 017, India
Penguin Group (NZ), 67 Apollo Drive, Rosedale, North Shore 0632, New Zealand
(a division of Pearson New Zealand Ltd)
Penguin Books (South Africa) (Pty) Ltd, 24 Sturdee Avenue, Rosebank, Johannesburg 2196, South Africa

Penguin Books Ltd, Registered Offices: 80 Strand, London WC2R 0RL, England

www.penguin.com

'The Work of Art in the Age of Mechanical Reproduction' first published 1936
'Franz Kafka' first published 1934
'Picturing Proust' first published 1929
This translation first published 2008

008

Translation copyright © J. A. Underwood, 2008
All rights reserved

The moral right of the translator has been asserted

Set by Rowland Phototypesetting Ltd, Bury St Edmunds, Suffolk
Printed in England by Clays Ltd, St Ives plc

978–0–141–03619–9

www.greenpenguin.co.uk

ALWAYS LEARNING   PEARSON

Contents

The Work of Art in the Age of Mechanical Reproduction

The establishment of the fine arts and their division into various categories go back to a time that differed radically from ours and to people whose power over things and circumstances was minute in comparison with our own. However, the astounding growth that our resources have undergone in terms of their precision and adaptability will in the near future confront us with very radical changes indeed in the ancient industry of the beautiful. In all arts there is a physical component that cannot continue to be considered and treated in the same way as before; no longer can it escape the effects of modern knowledge and modern practice. Neither matter nor space nor time is what, up until twenty years ago, it always was. We must be prepared for such profound changes to alter the entire technological aspect of the arts, influencing invention itself as a result, and eventually, it may be, contriving to alter the very concept of art in the most magical fashion.

Paul Valéry, *Pièces sur l'art*

Foreword

When Marx set out to analyse the capitalist mode of production, that mode of production was in its infancy.

Marx so ordered his endeavours that they acquired prognosticative value. Looking back at the basic circumstances of capitalist production, he presented them in such a way as to show what capitalism might be thought capable of in years to come. What emerged was that it might not only be thought capable of increasingly severe exploitation of proletarians; ultimately, it may even bring about conditions in which it can itself be done away with.

The transformation of the superstructure, which proceeds far more slowly than that of the substructure, has taken more than half a century to bring out the change in the conditions of production in all spheres of civilization. Only now can the form that this has assumed be revealed. Of those revelations, certain prognosticative demands need to be made. However, such demands will be met not so much by propositions concerning the art of the proletariat after it has seized power, let alone that of the classless society, as by propositions concerning how art will tend to develop under current conditions of production. The dialectic of those propositions makes itself no less apparent in the superstructure than in the economy. It would be wrong, therefore, to underestimate the combative value of such propositions. They oust a number of traditional concepts – such as creativity and genius, everlasting value and secrecy – concepts whose uncontrolled (and at the moment scarcely controllable) application leads to a processing of the facts along the lines of Fascism. *The following concepts, here introduced into art theory for the first time, differ from more familiar ones in that they are quite useless for the purposes of Fascism. They can, on the other hand, be used to formulate revolutionary demands in the politics of art.*

I

In principle, the work of art has always been reproducible. What man has made, man has always been able to make again. Such copying was also done by pupils as an artistic exercise, by masters in order to give works wider circulation, ultimately by anyone seeking to make money. Technological reproduction of the work of art is something else, something that has been practised intermittently throughout history, at widely separated intervals though with growing intensity. The Greeks had only two processes for reproducing works of art technologically: casting and embossing. Bronzes, terra-cottas and coins were the only artworks that they were able to manufacture in large numbers. All the rest were unique and not capable of being reproduced by techno-logical means. It was wood engraving that made graphic art technologically reproducible for the first time; draw-ings could be reproduced long before printing did the same for the written word. The huge changes that print-ing (the technological reproducibility of writing) brought about in literature are well known. However, of *the* phenomenon that we are considering on the scale of history here they are merely *a* particular instance – though of course a particularly important one. Wood engraving is joined in the course of the Middle Ages by copperplate engraving and etching, then in the early nineteenth century by lithography.

With lithography, reproductive technology reaches a radically new stage. The very much speedier process represented by applying a drawing to a stone as opposed to carving it into a block of wood or etching it onto a copperplate enabled graphic art, for the first time, to market its products not only in great numbers (as previously) but also in different designs daily. Lithography made it possible for graphic art to accompany everyday life with pictures. It started to keep pace with printing. However, in these early days it was outstripped, mere decades after the invention of lithography, by photography. With photography, in the process of pictorial reproduction the hand was for the first time relieved of the principal artistic responsibilities, which henceforth lay with the eye alone as it peered into the lens. Since the eye perceives faster than the hand can draw, the process of pictorial reproduction was so enormously speeded up that it was able to keep pace with speech. The film operator, turning the handle in the studio, captures the images as rapidly as the actor speaks. Whilst in lithography the illustrated magazine was present in essence, in photography it was the sound film. The technological reproduction of sound was tackled at the end of the last [nineteenth] century. These convergent endeavours rendered foreseeable a situation that Paul Valéry described in the sentence: 'Just as water, gas and electric power come to us from afar and enter our homes with almost no effort on our part, there serving our needs, so we shall be supplied with pictures or sound sequences that, at the touch of a button, almost a wave of the hand, arrive and likewise depart.' *Around 1900 technological reproduction had reached a standard at which it had not merely begun to take the totality of traditional artworks as its province, imposing the most profound changes on the impact of such works; it had even gained a place for itself among artistic modes of procedure.* As regards studying that standard, nothing is more revealing than how its twin manifestations – reproduction of the work of art and the new art of cinematography – redound upon art in its traditional form.

II

Even with the most perfect reproduction, *one thing* stands out: the here and now of the work of art – its unique existence in the place where it is at this moment. But it is on that unique existence and on nothing else that the history has been played out to which during the course of its being it has been subject. That includes not only the changes it has undergone in its physical structure over the course of time; it also includes the fluctuating conditions of ownership through which it may have passed.[1] The trace of the former will be brought to light only by chemical or physical analyses that cannot be carried out on a reproduction; that of the latter forms the object of a tradition, pursuit of which has to begin from the location of the original.

The here and now of the original constitute the abstract idea of its genuineness. Analyses of a chemical nature carried out on the patina of a bronze may help to establish its genuineness; similarly, proof that a particular medieval manuscript stems from a fifteenth-century archive may help to establish its genuineness. *The whole province of genuineness is beyond technological (and of course not only technological) reproducibility.*[2] But while in relation to manual reproduction (the product of which was usually branded a forgery of the original) the genuine article keeps its full authority, in relation to reproduction by technological means that is not the case. The reason is twofold. In the first place, a technological reproduction is more autonomous, relative to the original, than one made by hand. Through photography, for instance, it is able to bring out aspects of the original that can be accessed only by the lens (adjustable and selecting its viewpoint arbitrarily) and not by the human eye, or it is able to employ such techniques as enlargement or slow motion to capture images that are quite simply beyond natural optics. That is the first reason. Secondly, it can also place the copy of the original in situations beyond the reach of the original itself. Above all, it makes it possible for the original to come closer to the person taking it in, whether in the form of a photograph or in that of a gramophone record. A cathedral quits its site to find a welcome in the studio of an art lover; a choral work performed in a hall or in the open air can be heard in a room.

Even if the circumstances into which the product of technological reproduction of the work of art may be introduced in no way impair the continued existence of the work otherwise, its here and now will in any case be devalued. And if that by no means applies to the work of art alone but also, *mutatis mutandis*, to a landscape (for instance) that in a film slides past the viewer, as a result of that process a supremely sensitive core in the art object is affected that no natural object possesses in the same degree of vulnerability. That is its genuineness. The genuineness of a thing is the quintessence of everything about it since its creation that can be handed down, from its material duration to the historical witness that it bears. The latter (material duration and historical witness) being grounded in the former (the thing's genuineness), what happens in the reproduction, where the former has been removed from human perception, is that the latter also starts to wobble. Nothing else, admittedly; however, what starts to wobble thus is the authority of the thing.[3]

We can encapsulate what stands out here by using the term 'aura'. We can say: what shrinks in an age where the work of art can be reproduced by technological means is its aura. The process is symptomatic; its significance points beyond the realm of art. *Reproductive technology, we might say in general terms, removes the thing reproduced from the realm of tradition. In making many copies of the reproduction, it substitutes for its unique incidence a multiplicity of incidences. And in allowing the reproduction to come closer to whatever situation the person apprehending it is in, it actualizes what is reproduced.* These two processes usher in a mighty upheaval of what is passed on – an upheaval of tradition that is the verso of the current crisis and renewal of mankind. They are intimately bound up with the mass movements of our day. Their most powerful agent is film. Even in its most positive form (indeed, precisely therein), the social significance of film is unthinkable without this destructive, this cathartic side: namely, liquidation of the value of tradition in the cultural heritage. This phenomenon is at its most tangible in major historical films. It is drawing more and more positions into its sphere. And when Abel Gance exclaimed excitedly in 1927: 'Shakespeare, Rembrandt, Beethoven will make films [. . .] All legends, all mythologies and all myths, all founders of religions – all religions, indeed [. . .] await their filmed resurrection, and the heroes are pressing at the gates,' he was calling (doubtless without meaning to) for a comprehensive liquidation.

III

Within major historical periods, along with changes in the overall mode of being of the human collective, there are also changes in the manner of its sense perception. The manner in which human sense perception is organized, the medium in which it occurs, is dictated not only naturally but also historically. The time of the migration of peoples, in which the late-Roman art industry and the Vienna *Genesis* came into being, had not only a different art from the Ancient World but also a different perception. The scholars of the Vienna School, Riegl and Wickhoff, who rebelled against the weight of the classical tradition beneath which the art of that period lay buried, were the first to hit on the idea of drawing from that tradition inferences regarding the organization of perception in the age when it enjoyed currency. Far-reaching though their findings were, they were limited by the fact that these researchers contented themselves with revealing the formal signature that characterized perception in the late-Roman period. They did not try (and possibly could not even aspire) to reveal the social upheavals that found expression in those changes of perception. So far as the present is concerned, conditions are more favourable to such an insight. And if changes in the medium of perception occurring in our own day may be understood as a fading of aura, the social conditions of that fading can be demonstrated.

Perhaps we should illustrate the term 'aura' as proposed above for historical objects by the concept of an 'aura' of natural objects. The latter we define as a unique manifestation of a remoteness, however close it may be. Lying back on a summer's afternoon, gazing at a mountain range on the horizon or watching a branch as it casts its shadow over our reclining limbs, we speak of breathing in the aura of those mountains or that branch. It is not hard, given such a description, to see how much the current fading of aura depends upon social conditions. That fading has to do with two circumstances, both of which are connected with the increasing significance of the masses in present-day life. The fact is: *'Getting closer to things' in both spatial and human terms is every bit as passionate a concern of today's masses* [4] *as their tendency to surmount the uniqueness of each circumstance by seeing it in reproduction.* There is no denying that we see evidence every day of the need to apprehend objects in pictures (or rather in copies, in reproductions of pictures) from very close to. And there is no mistaking the difference between the reproduction (such as illustrated papers and weekly news round-ups hold in readiness) and the picture. Uniqueness and duration are as tightly intertwined in the latter as are transience and reiterability in the former. Stripping the object of its sheath, shattering the aura, bear witness to a kind of perception where 'a sense of similarity in the world' is so highly developed that, through reproduction, it even mines similarity from what only happens once. For instance, we are starting to see in the visual field what in the field of theory is emerging as the growing importance of statistics. The orientation of reality toward the masses and of the masses toward reality is a process of unbounded consequence not only for thought but also for the way we see things.

IV

The uniqueness of the work of art is identical with its embeddedness in the context of tradition. Tradition itself is of course something very much alive, something extraordinarily changeable. A classical statue of Venus, for example, occupied a different traditional context for the Greeks, who made of it an object of worship, than for medieval clerics, who saw it as a threatening idol. But what both were equally struck by was its singularity or, to use another word, its aura. The original way in which the work of art was embedded in the context of tradition was through worship. The oldest works of art, as we know, came into being in the service of some ritual – magical at first, then religious. Now it is crucially important that this auric mode of being of the work of art never becomes completely separated from its ritual function.[5] To put it another way: *The 'one-of-a-kind' value of the 'genuine' work of art has its underpinnings in the ritual in which it had its original, initial utility value.* No matter how indirectly, this is still recognizable even in the most profane forms of the service of beauty as a secularized rite.[6] The profane service of beauty that emerged with the Renaissance and remained significant for three hundred years thereafter did eventually, at the end of that time, following the first major upheaval to assail it, clearly reveal those foundations. What happened was: when, with the advent of the first truly revolutionary means of reproduction, namely photography (simultaneously with the dawn of Socialism), art felt a crisis approaching that after a further century became unmistakable, it reacted with the theory of '*l'art pour l'art*' ['art for art's sake'], which constitutes a theology of art. From it there proceeded, in the further course of events, almost a negative theology in the form of the idea of a 'pure' art that rejected not only any kind of social function but also any prompting by an actual subject. (In poetry, Mallarmé was the first to reach this position.)

Paying proper attention to these circumstances is indispensable for a view of art that has to do with the work of art in an age when it can be reproduced by technological means. The reason is that they herald what is here the crucial insight: its being reproducible by technological means frees the work of art, for the first time in history, from its existence as a parasite upon ritual. The reproduced work of art is to an ever-increasing extent the reproduction of a work of art designed for reproducibility.[7] From a photographic plate, for instance, many prints can be made; the question of the genuine print has no meaning. *However, the instant the criterion of genuineness in art production failed, the entire social function of art underwent an upheaval. Rather than being underpinned by ritual, it came to be underpinned by a different practice: politics.*

V

Works of art are received and appreciated with different points of emphasis, two of which stand out as being poles of each other. In one case the emphasis is on the work's cultic value; in the other, on its display value.[8,9] Artistic production begins with images that serve cultic purposes. With such images, presumably, their presence is more important than the fact that they are seen. The elk depicted by the Stone Age man on the walls of his cave is an instrument of magic. Yes, he shows it to his fellows, but it is chiefly targeted at spirits. Today this cultic value as such seems almost to insist that the work of art be kept concealed: certain god statues are accessible only to the priest in the *cella*, certain Madonna images remain veiled almost throughout the year, certain carvings on medieval cathedrals cannot be seen by the spectator at ground level. *As individual instances of artistic production become emancipated from the context of religious ritual, opportunities for displaying the products increase.* The 'displayability' of a portrait bust, which is capable of being dispatched hither and thither, exceeds that of a god statue, whose fixed place is inside the temple. The displayability of the panel painting is greater than that of the mosaic or fresco that preceded it. And if a setting of the mass is not inherently any less displayable than a symphony, nevertheless the symphony emerged at the point in time when it looked like becoming more so than the mass.

With the various methods of reproducing the work of art by technological means, this displayability increases so enormously that the quantitative shift between its two poles switches, as in primeval times, to become a qualitative change of nature. In primeval times, because of the absolute weight placed on its cultic value, the work of art became primarily an instrument of magic that was only subsequently, one might say, acknowledged to be a work of art. Today, in the same way, because of the absolute weight placed on its display value, the work of art is becoming an image with entirely new functions, of which the one we are aware of, namely the artistic function, stands out as one that may subsequently be deemed incidental.[10] This much is certain, that currently photography and its issue, film, provide the most practical implementation of this discovery.

VI

In photography, display value starts to drive cultic value back along the whole line. However, cultic value does not give ground without resistance. It occupies one last ditch, and that is the human face. It is no accident, not at all, that the portrait forms the centrepiece of early photography. In the cult of recalling absent or dead loved ones, the cultic value of the image finds its last refuge. In the transient expression of a human countenance in early photographs, we catch one final glimpse of aura. It is this that gives them their melancholic, matchless beauty. But where the human form withdraws from photography, there for the first time display value gets the better of cultic value. And it is having set the scene for this process to occur that gives Atget, the man who captured so many deserted Parisian streets around 1900, his incomparable significance. Quite rightly it has been said of him that he recorded those streets like crime scenes. A crime scene, too, is deserted. Atget snaps clues. With Atget, photographs become exhibits in the trial that is history. That is what constitutes their hidden political significance. They already call for a specific type of reception. Free-floating contemplation is no longer an appropriate reaction here. They unsettle the viewer; he feels obliged to find a specific way of approaching them. At the same time the illustrated journals start to erect signposts, suggesting that way. Right or wrong – no matter. In them the caption first became obligatory. And clearly this possessed a quite different character than the title of a painting. Shortly afterwards, the directives that the viewer of pictures in the illustrated press receives via the caption become even more precise and imperious in film, where the way in which each individual image is apprehended appears to be dictated by the sequence of all that have gone before.

VII

The clash fought out during the nineteenth century as painting and photography disputed the artistic merits of their respective products seems muddled and ill-conceived today. However, far from denying its importance, this may actually underline it. The fact is, that clash was the expression of a historical upheaval of which, as such, neither party was aware. The age where art became reproducible by technological means, in setting it free from its cultic roots, extinguished the light of its autonomy for ever. Yet the alteration in the function of art thus engendered dropped from the century's field of view. And even the succeeding century, the twentieth, which saw the development of film, long remained oblivious to it.

Much wisdom had already been thrown away on trying to decide whether photography was an art (without asking the prior question: whether, with the invention of photography, the very nature of art had undergone a change), but before long the theoreticians of film were asking a similarly hasty question. However, the problems that photography had presented for traditional aesthetics were child's play compared to what film had in store. Hence the blind violence that marked the beginnings of film criticism. Here is Abel Gance, for instance, likening film to hieroglyphics: 'This has then brought us, in the wake of a most remarkable return to the past, back to the level of expression of the Egyptians [. . .]. Pictography has not yet reached full maturity for the reason that our eyes are not yet up to it. There is not yet enough respect, not enough *cult* for what seeks expression through it.' Or as Séverin-Mars writes: 'What art was ever granted a dream that [. . .] was more poetic and at the same time more real! Looked at from that standpoint, film would represent a form of expression entirely beyond compare, and only persons of the noblest way of thinking in the most sublime, most mysterious moments of their careers might be permitted to move within its atmosphere.' As for Alexandre Arnoux, he roundly concludes a fantasy on silent film with the question: 'All the bold descriptions we have made use of here – ought they not without exception to add up to how we define prayer?' It is most instructive to see how the endeavour to annex film to 'art' requires such critics to throw caution to the winds in reading cultic elements into their subject. And yet, by the time these speculations appeared, such works as *A Woman of Paris* and *The Gold Rush* had already been made. That does not stop Abel Gance from invoking his comparison with hieroglyphics, and Séverin-Mars talks of film as one might discuss the paintings of Fra Angelico. What is characteristic is that, still today [i.e. 1936], particularly reactionary writers seek the meaning of film along the same lines, finding it not in the sacred, perhaps, but certainly in the supernatural. When Reinhardt made his [1935] film of *A Midsummer Night's Dream*, Werfel observed that it was undoubtedly sterile imitation of the external world with its streets, interiors, railway stations, restaurants, cars and beaches that had hitherto prevented film from soaring into the realms of art. 'Film has not yet attained its real meaning or seized its true potential [. . .]. These consist in its unique ability to give voice, using natural means in an incomparably persuasive manner, to the fairy-like, the miraculous, the super-natural.'

VIII

The artistic performance of the stage actor [i.e. what he or she *does* artistically] is presented to the audience by the actor in person; of that there is no doubt. The artistic performance of the screen actor, on the other hand, is presented to the audience via a piece of equipment, a film camera. The latter has two consequences. The apparatus that mediates the performance of the screen actor to the audience is not obliged to respect that performance as an entity. Guided by its operator, the camera comments on the performance continuously. The outcome of that running commentary, which the editor then assembles from material supplied, is the film as finally put together. It includes a certain number of movements that need to be recognized as those of the camera itself – not to mention such special settings as close-ups. The screen actor's performance thus undergoes a series of optical tests. This is the first consequence of the state of affairs arising out of the fact that the screen actor's performance is mediated by the camera. The second consequence is that the screen actor, by not presenting his performance to the audience in person, is deprived of the possibility open to the stage actor of adapting that performance to the audience as the show goes on; the cinema audience is being asked to examine and report without any personal contact with the performer intruding. *The audience empathizes with the performer only by empathizing with the camera. It thus assumes the camera's stance: it tests.*[11] This is not a stance from which cultic value can be judged.

IX

Film is very much less interested in having the actor portray another person to the audience than in having the actor portray himself to the camera. One of the first people to sense this transformation of the actor as a result of performance-as-test was Pirandello. It detracts only slightly from the comments he makes in this connection in his novel *Shoot* that they confine themselves to stressing the negative aspect of the matter. Even less that they relate to silent films. Because the sound film did nothing fundamental to alter things in this respect. The fact remains, the acting concerned is done for a piece of equipment – or, in the case of the sound film, for two. 'The screen actor,' Pirandello writes, 'feels as if exiled. Exiled not only from the stage but from his own person.

With dim disquiet he senses the inexplicable emptiness that results from his body becoming a withdrawal symptom, from its dissipating and being robbed of its reality, its life, its voice, and the sounds it makes by moving around, reduced to a mute image that flickers on the screen for an instant, then disappears into thin air [. . .]. The little projector will play with his shadow before the audience; and he himself must be content to act in front of the camera.' That same state of affairs may be described as follows: for the first time (and it is film that has done this) a person is placed in the position, while operating with his whole being, of having to dispense with the aura that goes with it. For that aura is bound to his here and now; it has no replica. The aura surrounding Macbeth onstage cannot, for the live audience, be detached from the aura that surrounds the actor playing him. But what is peculiar about filming in the studio is that in the latter situation the audience is replaced by a piece of equipment. The aura surrounding the player must thus be lost – and with it, at the same time, the aura around the character played.

That it should be precisely a dramatist (Pirandello) who instinctively identifies the distinguishing characteristic of film as causing the crisis we see befalling the theatre comes as no surprise. A work of art captured entirely by technological reproduction, indeed (like film) proceeding from it, can have no more direct opposite than live theatre. Every more detailed examination confirms this. Expert observers long since acknowledged that in film 'it happens almost invariably that the greatest effects are achieved when the least "acting" is done

[. . .]. The ultimate development being [according to Arnheim, writing in 1932] to treat the actor as a prop that is selected for character and [. . .] put to use in the right place.'[12] There is something else very closely bound up with this. *An actor working in the theatre enters into a part. Very often, the screen actor is not allowed to.* The latter's performance is not a single entity; it consists of many individual performances. Along with such incidental considerations as studio hire, availability of partners, setting and so on, basic mechanical requirements break the screen actor's performance down into a series of episodes that can then be assembled. One thinks above all of lighting, installing which means that portrayal of a process that appears on the screen as a single rapid sequence of events must be captured in a series of individual shots that may, in the studio, extend over hours. Not to mention more palpable montages. A leap from a window may, in the studio, be filmed as a leap from scaffolding, while the subsequent flight may be filmed weeks later, during an outside shoot. Nor is it difficult to construe even more paradoxical instances. Possibly, following a knock at the door, an actor is asked to start in surprise. His reaction may turn out to be unsatisfactory. In which case the director may resort to arranging, one day when the actor happens to be back in the studio, for a gun to be fired behind him without warning. The shock registered by the actor at that moment may be captured and later edited into the film. Nothing shows more graphically that art has escaped from the realm of the 'beautiful pretence', which for so long was deemed the only habitat in which it might thrive.

X

The actor's alienation in front of the film camera, as Pirandello describes it, is inherently of the same sort as a person's feeling of surprise and displeasure when confronted with his mirror-image. Now, however, the reflection can be separated from the person; it has become transportable. And where is it transported to? Before an audience.[13] Awareness of this never leaves the screen actor, not for a moment. *The screen actor is conscious, all the while he is before the camera, that in the final analysis he is dealing with the audience: the audience of consumers who constitute the market.* That market, which he is entering not merely with his labour but with his very presence, his entire physical being, is quite as intangible, so far as he is concerned at the time of the performance aimed at it, as is any article produced in a factory. Surely that fact is going to heighten the sense of unease engendered by the new fear that, according to Pirandello, comes over the actor facing a film camera? Film's response to the shrivelling of aura is an artificial inflation of 'personality' outside the studio. The cult of stardom promoted by film capital preserves the magic of personality that for years has lain solely in the rancid magic of its commodity character. While film capital sets the tone, no other revolutionary service can be ascribed to present-day film in general than that of furthering a revolutionary critique of traditional notions of art. Certainly, in particular instances film today may go beyond that, furthering a revolutionary critique of social conditions, indeed of the property order. But that is no more the burden of the present investigation than it is the burden of film production in western Europe.

One concomitant of cinematographic technology, as of sporting technology, is that everyone watches the performances displayed as a semi-expert. If you have ever heard a group of newspaper boys, leaning on their bikes, discussing the results of a cycle race, you will have some understanding of this state of affairs. It is with good reason that newspaper publishers organize competitive events for their young delivery staff. These tournaments arouse great interest among participants, the reason being that the victor of such an event has the chance of rising from newspaper boy to racing cyclist. Similarly the weekly newsreel, for example, gives everyone an opportunity to rise from passer-by to film extra. He may even, in this way, find himself transported into a work of art (think of Vertov's *Three Songs about Lenin* or Ivens's *Borinage*). *All persons today can stake a claim to being filmed.* That claim is best explained by a glance at the historical situation of current literature.

For centuries the situation in literature was such that a small number of writers faced many thousands of times that number of readers. Then, towards the end of the last century, there came a change. As the press grew in volume, making ever-increasing numbers of new political, religious, scientific, professional and local organs available to its readership, larger and larger sections of that readership (gradually, at first) turned into writers. It began with the daily newspapers opening their 'correspondence columns' to such people, and it has now reached a point where few Europeans involved in the labour process could fail, basically, to find some opportunity or other to publish an experience at work, a complaint, a piece of reporting or something similar. The distinction between writer and readership is thus in the process of losing its fundamental character. That distinction is becoming a functional one, assuming a different form from one case to the next. The reader is constantly ready to become a writer. As an expert, which for good or ill he must inevitably become in a highly specialized labour process (be it merely an expert in some minor matter), he gains access to authorship. In the Soviet Union, labour itself has a voice. And putting one's job into words is part of the skill required to perform it. Literary authority is no longer grounded in specialist education but in polytechnic education; it has become common property.[14]

All of which can easily be translated into terms of film, where shifts that in literature took centuries have occurred within a decade. For in film (particularly as practised in Russia) this sort of shift has already, in places, been accomplished. Some of the actors encountered in Russian films are not actors in our sense but people who portray *themselves* (and do so primarily through their labour). In western Europe, capitalist exploitation of film bars modern man's legitimate claim to be reproduced from being taken into consideration. Given the circumstances, the film industry has every interest in arousing the participation of the masses by means of illusory presentations and suggestive speculations.

XI

A film, particularly a sound film, affords the kind of spectacle that was never before conceivable, not at any time nor in any place. It portrays an event that can no longer be assigned to a single standpoint from which things not strictly belonging to the performance process as such (camera, lighting equipment, crew and so on) would not fall within the spectator's field of view. (Unless, that is, the pupil of his eye shared the setting of the camera lens.) This fact, more than any other, renders any similarities that may exist between a scene in the film studio and a scene onstage superficial and quite unimportant. Live theatre is aware as a matter of principle of the point from which what is happening cannot simply be seen through as illusory. When, on the other hand, a film is being made, no such point exists. The illusory nature of film is a second-tier nature; it derives from editing. What this means is: *In the film studio the camera has penetrated so deeply into reality that the pure aspect of the latter, uncontaminated by the camera, emerges from a special procedure, namely being shot by a piece of photographic equipment specifically adapted for the purpose and then pasted together with other shots of the same kind.* The camera-free aspect of reality is here at its most artificial, and the sight of what is actually going on has become the blue flower [of Romanticism] in the land of technology.

The same state of affairs as here contrasts with that obtaining in the theatre can even more revealingly be compared to that which informs painting. In this case the question we need to ask is: how does the cameraman relate to the painter? To answer it, perhaps I may be permitted an auxiliary construction based on the concept of the *Operateur* [the now-obsolete German term for the film-crew member Benjamin clearly has in mind] as we are familiar with it in connection with surgery. The surgeon constitutes one pole of an arrangement in which the other is occupied by the magician. The stance of the magician healing an invalid by laying-on of hands differs from that of the surgeon performing an operation on that invalid. The magician maintains the natural distance between himself and the patient; to be precise, he reduces it only slightly (by virtue of a laying-on of hands) while increasing it (by virtue of his authority) hugely. The surgeon does the opposite: he reduces the distance to the patient a great deal (by actually going inside him) and increases it only a little (through the care with which his hand moves among the latter's organs). In short, unlike the magician (still a latent presence in the medical practitioner), the surgeon abstains at the crucial moment from facing his invalid person to person, invading him surgically instead.

Magician and surgeon behave like painter and cameraman. The painter, while working, observes a natural distance from the subject; the cameraman, on the other hand, penetrates deep into the subject's tissue.[15] The images they both come up with are enormously different. The painter's is an entity, the cameraman's chopped up into a large number of pieces, which find their way back together by following a new law. *That is why the filmic portrayal of reality is of such incomparably greater significance to people today, because it continues to provide the camera-free aspect of reality that they are entitled to demand of a work of art precisely by using the camera to penetrate that reality so thoroughly.*

XII

The fact that the work of art can now be reproduced by technological means alters the relationship of the mass to art. From being very backward (faced with a Picasso, for instance), it has become extremely progressive (given Chaplin, for instance). Yet this progressive response is characterized by the fact that in it the pleasure of looking and experiencing is associated, directly and profoundly, with the stance of passing an expert judgement. This link is an important social indicator. In fact, the more the social significance of an art diminishes, the greater the extent (as is clearly turning out to be the case with painting) to which the critical and pleasure-seeking stances of the public diverge. The conventional is enjoyed without criticism, the truly new is criticized with aversion. In the cinema, the critical and pleasure-seeking stances of the audience coincide. And what crucially makes this happen is: nowhere more than in the cinema do the individual reactions that together make up the mass reaction of the audience prove from the outset to be caused by their immediately imminent massing. And in making themselves heard, they also check on one another. Again, painting offers a useful comparison here. A painting always had an excellent claim to being looked at by one person or a small number. The kind of simultaneous viewing of paintings by large crowds that occurs in the nineteenth century is an early symptom of the crisis affecting painting, which was certainly not triggered by photography alone but, relatively independently of photography, by the work of art laying claim to mass attention.

The fact is, painting is not able to form the object of simultaneous reception by large numbers of people, as architecture has always been, as the epic once was, and as film is today. And despite the inherent impossibility of drawing conclusions from that fact regarding the social role of painting, the same fact nevertheless counts as a severe setback at a time when painting, as a result of special circumstances and to some extent in defiance of its nature, finds itself face to face with the masses. In the churches and monasteries of the Middle Ages and in the palaces of princes up until the late eighteenth century, joint reception of paintings occurred not simultaneously but often in stages, when it was handed down hierarchically. Where this happened otherwise, what comes out is the special conflict that befell painting as a result of the image becoming reproducible by technological means. But although an attempt was made to bring painting before the masses in galleries and salons, there was no way in which the masses could have organized and checked on themselves in the context of that kind of reception.[16] As a result, the same audience as reacts in a progressive fashion to a grotesque film will inevitably, in the presence of Surrealism, become a backward one.

XIII

The distinguishing features of film lie not only in the way in which man presents himself to the camera but in how, using the camera, he presents his surroundings to himself. A glance at performance psychology will illustrate the camera's ability to test. A glance at psychoanalysis will illustrate a different aspect of that ability. Film has indeed enriched our perceptual world with methods that can be illustrated by those of Freudian theory. Fifty years ago, a conversational slip went more or less unnoticed. Its suddenly revealing depths in what had previously seemed a superficial discussion was probably regarded as an exception. Since *The Psychopathology of Everyday Life* [1901], that has changed. The book isolated and at the same time made susceptible of analysis things that had once swept past unnoticed in the broad stream of things perceived. Film has resulted in a similar deepening of apperception across the whole optical (and now also acoustic) segment of the sensory world. It is simply the reverse side of this state of affairs that performances presented in film can be analysed more exactly and from many more angles than can performances expressed in paint or onstage. Compared with painting, it is the infinitely more detailed presentation of the situation that gives the performance portrayed on the screen its greater analysability. Compared with live theatre, the greater analysability of the performance portrayed cinematically is due to a higher degree of isolatability. That fact (and this is its chief significance) tends to foster the interpenetration of art and science. Indeed, in connection with a piece of behaviour embedded in a specific situation and now (like a muscle from a cadaver) neatly dissected out, it can scarcely be said which is more gripping: its artistic worth or its scientific usefulness. *It will count among the revolutionary functions of film that it renders the artistic and scientific uses of photography, which beforehand generally diverged, recognizably identical.*[17]

By choosing close-ups from stock, accentuating hidden details of props with which we are familiar, exploring commonplace environments under the inspired guidance of the lens, on the one hand film increases our understanding of the inevitabilities that govern our lives while ensuring, on the other hand, that we have a vast, undreamt-of amount of room for manoeuvre! Our pubs and city streets, our offices and furnished rooms, our factories and railway stations seemed desperately imprisoning. Then film came along and exploded all these dungeons with the dynamite of its tenths of a second, leaving us free, now, to undertake adventurous journeys amid their widely scattered ruins. The close-up expands space as the slow-motion sequence dilates movement. And just as enlargement is not really concerned with simply clarifying what we glimpse 'anyway' but rather brings out wholly new structural formations in matter, neither does the slow-motion technique simply bring out familiar movement motifs but reveals in them others that are quite unfamiliar and that 'bear no resemblance to decelerations of rapid movements but are like strangely gliding, floating, supernatural ones'. Palpably, then, this is a different nature that addresses the camera than the one that speaks to the eye. Different above all in that the space permeated by human consciousness is replaced by one that is unconsciously permeated. While it is quite normal for a person to draw conclusions, even if only in outline, from the way others walk, that person will certainly know nothing of the walkers' posture in the split second of their stepping out. And if we have a rough idea of how we pick up a cigarette lighter or a spoon, we know little of what actually happens between hand and metal when we do so, not to mention how this will vary according to our current mood. Here the camera intervenes with its different aids, its plunging and soaring, its interrupting and isolating, its stretching and condensing of the process, its close-ups and its distance shots. Only the camera can show us the optical unconscious, as it is only through psychoanalysis that we learn of the compulsive unconscious.

XIV

It has always been among art's most important functions to generate a demand for whose full satisfaction the time has not yet come.[18] The history of every art form has critical periods in which that form strives for effects that are able to find expression without effort only when technology has reached a new level – that is to say, in a new art form. The flamboyance, even crudeness, that art manifests in this way, especially in what are called 'periods of decadence', spring in fact from art's richest core of historical forces. Latterly, Dadaism revelled in such barbarisms. Only now is what drove it becoming clear: *Dadaism was trying to generate the effects that people now look for in film, but using the tools of painting (sometimes literature).*

Any radically new, pioneering generation of demands will go too far. Dadaism does so to the point of sacrificing the market values that film possesses in such abundance in favour of more significant intentions – of which it was not, of course, aware in the form we have been describing. The commercial marketability of their works of art meant far less to the Dadaists than their non-marketability as objects of contemplative immersion. They sought to achieve that non-marketability, that unrealizable quality, not least by fundamentally disparaging their material. Their poems are 'word-salad', containing obscene expressions and all manner of linguistic detritus. Likewise their paintings, onto which they glued buttons or bus tickets. What they achieve by such means is the ruthless destruction of the aura of their output, which they use the means of production to stamp as 'reproduction'. It is impossible, in the presence of a picture by Arp or a poem by August Stramm, to take time out, as one can with a Derain painting or a Rilke poem, for contemplation and for forming a view. Immersion, which in the degeneration of the bourgeoisie became a school of asocial behaviour, stands over against diversion as a variety of social behaviour.[19] Dadaist demonstrations did indeed constitute a very violent diversion in that they placed the work of art at the centre of a scandal. That work had above all to meet *one* requirement: it must provoke public irritation.

In the hands of the Dadaists the work of art, from being a sight that seduced the eye or a sound that persuaded the ear, became a bullet. It flew towards the viewer, striking him down. It assumed a tactile quality. In so doing, it furthered the demand for film, the distracting element of which is also a mainly tactile element, being based on changes of setting and camera angle that stab the viewer with repeated thrusts. Compare, if you will, the screen on which the film unrolls to the canvas that carries the painting. The latter invites the viewer to contemplate; he is able, in front of it, to give himself up to his chain of associations. Watching a film, he cannot do this. Scarcely has he set eyes on it before it is already different. It cannot be pinned down. Duhamel, who hates film and understands none of its importance, though he does know something about its structure, comments on this state of affairs as follows: 'I can no longer think what I wish to think. The moving images have ousted my thoughts.' The chain of associations of the person viewing those images is indeed instantly interrupted by their changing. That is what film's shock effect is based on, which like every shock effect seeks to be offset by heightened presence of mind.[20] *By virtue of its technical structure film has taken the wraps off the physical shock effect that Dadaism kept shrouded, as it were, in the moral sphere.*[21]

XV

The mass is a matrix from which currently all customary responses to works of art are springing newborn. Quantity has now become quality: *the very much greater masses of participants have produced a changed kind of participation.* The observer should not be put off by the fact that such participation initially appears in a disreputable form. There has been no shortage, in fact, of observers who have stuck passionately to precisely this superficial aspect of the matter. Of these, Duhamel has spoken most radically. What he blames film for mainly is the nature of the participation it arouses amongst the masses. He calls film 'a pastime for helots, a distraction for uneducated, wretched, overworked creatures who are consumed by their worries [. . .], a spectacle that requires no concentration of any kind, that presupposes no ability to think [. . .], lights no flame in people's hearts, and kindles no other sort of hope than the ludicrous one of becoming, at some time, a "star" in Los Angeles'. Clearly, this is at bottom the old charge that the masses are looking for distraction whereas art calls for immersion on the viewer's part. It is a platitude. Which leaves only the question: does this furnish an angle from which to study film? Here we need to take a closer look. Distraction and immersion constitute opposites, enabling us to say this: The person who stands in contemplation before a work of art immerses himself in it; he enters that work – as legend tells us happened to a Chinese painter on once catching sight of his finished painting. The distracted mass, on the other hand, absorbs the work of art into itself. Buildings, most obviously. Architecture has always provided the prototype of a work of art that is received in a state of distraction and by the collective. The laws governing its reception have most to tell us.

Buildings have been with mankind since its earliest history. Many forms of art have come and gone. Tragedy emerges with the Greeks, then disappears with them, to be revived centuries later only in accordance with its 'laws'. The epic, after originating in the youth of nations, wanes in Europe with the passing of the Renaissance. Panel painting is a creation of the Middle Ages; nothing guarantees that it will continue uninterrupted. But man's need for shelter is perennial. The art of building has never lain fallow. Its history is longer than that of any other art, and imaginatively recalling its effect is important as regards any attempt to form a conclusion about how the masses relate to art. Buildings are received twofold: through how they are used and how they are perceived. Or to put it a better way: in a tactile fashion and in an optical fashion. No idea of such reception is conveyed by imagining it as taking place collectedly – as is the case among tourists, for example, ogling famous buildings. The fact is, there is not, on the tactile side, any counterpart to what on the optical side constitutes contemplation. Tactile reception does not occur both through the medium of attentiveness and at the same time through that of habit. As regards architecture, the latter largely determines even optical reception. The truth of the matter is that this also tends to occur very much less in a state of close attention than in one of casual observation. However, there are circumstances in which this reception accorded to architecture possesses canonical value. Because: *The tasks that at times of great historical upheaval the human perceptual apparatus is asked to perform are simply not solvable by visual means alone –*

that is to say, through contemplation. They are gradually mastered, on the instructions of tactile reception, by man's getting used to them.

Getting used to things is something even the distracted person can do. More: the ability to master certain tasks in a state of distraction is what proves that solving them has become a person's habit. Through the sort of distraction that art has to offer, a surreptitious check is kept on how far fresh tasks of apperception have become solvable. Since, moreover, there is a temptation for individuals to duck such tasks, art will attack the most difficult and crucial of them where it is able to mobilize masses. It is currently doing so in film. *The kind of reception in a state of distraction that to an increasing extent is becoming apparent in all fields of art and is symptomatic of profound changes in apperception has its true practice instrument in film.* In its shock effect film goes halfway towards meeting this form of reception. Film pushes back cult value not only by persuading the audience to adopt an appraising stance but also by ensuring that this appraising stance in the cinema does not include attentiveness. The audience is an examiner, but a distracted one.

Afterword

The increasing proletarianization of people today and the increasing formation of masses are two sides of one and the same sequence of events. Fascism seeks to organize the newly emergent proletarianized masses without touching the property relations that those masses are so urgently trying to abolish. Fascism sees its salvation in allowing the masses to find their voice (not, of course, to receive their due).[22] The masses have a right to see the ownership structure changed: Fascism seeks to give them a *voice* in retaining that structure unaltered. *Fascism leads logically to an aestheticization of political life.* The violation of the masses, which in a leader cult it forces to their knees, corresponds to the violation exercised by a film camera, which Fascism enlists in the service of producing cultic values.

All efforts to aestheticize politics culminate in one point. That one point is war. War, and war only, makes it possible to give mass movements on a colossal scale a goal, while retaining the traditional ownership structure. That is how the situation looks from the political viewpoint. From the viewpoint of technology it looks like this: Only war makes it possible to mobilize all the technological resources of the present day while retaining the ownership structure. Obviously, the apotheosis of war by Fascism does not deploy *these* arguments. Nevertheless, a quick consideration of them will be instructive. In Marinetti's *Manifesto Concerning the Ethiopian Colonial War* we read: 'For twenty-seven years we Futurists have been objecting to the way war is described as anti-aesthetic [. . .]. Accordingly, we state: [. . .] War is beautiful because thanks to gas masks, terror-inducing megaphones, flame-throwers, and small tanks man's dominion over the subject machine is proven. War is beautiful because it ushers in the dreamt-of metallization of the human body. War is beautiful because it enriches a meadow in bloom by adding the fiery orchids of machine-guns. War is beautiful because it combines rifle-fire, barrages of bullets, lulls in the firing, and the scents and smells of putrescence into a symphony. War is beautiful because it creates fresh architectures such as those of the large tank, geometrical flying formations, spirals of smoke rising from burning villages, and much else besides [. . .]. Writers and artists of Futurism [. . .], remember these principles of an aesthetics of war in order that your struggles to find a new kind of poetry and a new kind of sculpture [. . .] may be illuminated thereby!'

This manifesto has the advantage of clarity. The questions it poses deserve to be adopted by the dialectician. It sees the aesthetics of modern warfare as follows: if natural exploitation of the forces of production is held back by the ownership structure, the increase in technological substitutes, tempi and sources of power calls urgently for unnatural exploitation. This it finds in war, which with its destructions affords proof that society was not sufficiently mature to make technology its organ, that technology was not sufficiently developed to cope with society's elemental forces. Imperialistic war is characterized in its ghastliest traits by the discrepancy between the hugely powerful means of production and their inadequate exploitation in the production process (in other words, by unemployment and lack of markets). *Imperialistic war is a rebellion on the part of a technology that is collecting in 'human material' the ambitions that society has robbed it of in terms of natural materials.* Rather than develop rivers into canals, it diverts the human stream to flow into the bed of its trenches; rather than scatter seeds from its aeroplanes, it drops incendiary bombs on cities; and in gas warfare it has found a new way of doing away with aura.

'*Fiat ars – pereat mundus*', says Fascism, looking (as Marinetti professes) to war for artistic satisfaction of the different kind of sensory perception brought about by technology. This is clearly the culmination of '*l'art pour l'art*' ['art for art's sake']. Humanity, which in Homer's day provided a spectacle for the gods of Olympus, has now become one for itself. Its alienation from itself has reached a point where it now allows its own destruction to be savoured as an aesthetic pleasure of the first order. *That is how things are, given the kind of aestheticization of politics that Fascism pursues. Communism's reply is to politicize art.*

Notes

1. It goes without saying that the history of the work of art embraces more: that of the *Mona Lisa*, for instance, includes the nature and number of the copies made of it in the seventeenth, eighteenth and nineteenth centuries.

2. Precisely because genuineness is not reproducible, intensive intrusion by certain reproductive processes (technological ones) provided a handle for differentiating and grading genuineness. Cultivating such distinctions was an important function of the art trade. This had an obvious interest in maintaining a separation between different prints from a wood block (those prior to and those sub-

sequent to printing), a copperplate, and the like. With the invention of wood engraving, the quality of genuineness was attacked at the root, so to speak, before it had produced its late flowering. 'Genuine' was something a medieval Madonna image was not at the time of its making – not yet; that was something it became over the course of ensuing centuries, most plentifully, perhaps, in the last [the nineteenth century].

3. The crummiest provincial performance of *Faust* nevertheless has this over a *Faust* film: notionally, it stands in competition with the first Weimar performance. And what, in terms of traditional content, the audience may recall across the footlights becomes unusable in the cinema (e.g. the fact that the character of Mephisto contains elements of a friend of Goethe's youth, Johann Heinrich Merck, and so on and so forth).

4. Bringing oneself closer to the masses in human terms may mean: having one's function in society removed from view. There is no guarantee that a present-day portraitist, painting a famous surgeon at breakfast or surrounded by his family, will capture the sitter's function in society more accurately than a sixteenth-century painter portraying his doctors to the public as imposing presences – as Rembrandt, for example, does in *The Anatomy Lesson*.

5. The definition of aura as 'a unique manifestation of a remoteness, no matter how near it may be' represents nothing other than a formulation of the cultic value of the work of art in categories of spatial and temporal perception. Remoteness is the opposite of propinquity. The *essence* of remoteness is that it cannot be approached. Indeed, unapproachability is one of the chief qualities of the cultic image. By its very nature, it remains 'remote

no matter how near'. Any propinquity lent by its embodi-
ment as matter does not impair the remoteness retained
from its constituting a manifestation.

6. The more the cultic value of the image is secularized, the
less specific ideas of the substratum of its uniqueness
become. To an ever-increasing extent, the uniqueness of
the phenomenon inhabiting the cultic image is driven out
by the empirical uniqueness of the artist or the artist's
creative achievement in the eye of the beholder. Never
in its entirety, of course; the concept of genuineness never
ceases to reach beyond that of authentic attribution. (This
comes out with especial clarity in the person of the
collector, who always has something of the slave to
fetishism about him and through possessing the work of
art partakes of its cultic power.) Nevertheless, the function
of the concept of authenticity in the contemplation of art
remains unambiguous: with the secularization of art,
authenticity supplants cultic value.

7. In connection with works of cinematography, the fact
that the product can be reproduced by technological
means is not (as with works of literature, for example, or
painting) a condition of its mass circulation imposed from
outside. *The technological reproducibility of films is rooted
directly in the manner of their production. This not merely
facilitates the mass circulation of films in the most direct way;
it positively necessitates it.* It necessitates it because a film
costs so much to produce that an individual who might
be able to afford a painting, for instance, cannot afford
the former. In 1927 someone worked out that a major
film, if it was to pay for itself, had to reach an audience
of nine million. With sound films, of course, things took
a step backwards at first; the audience for 'talkies' was
limited by language barriers, and this occurred at the

same time as Fascism was laying such stress on national interests. However, more important than recording this setback (which in any case dubbing diminished) is considering its connection with Fascism. The fact that the two phenomena emerged at the same time has to do with the economic crisis. The same disturbances as, viewed on a grand scale, led to the attempt to preserve the existing conditions of ownership by means of open violence led the film capital threatened by the crisis to force the pace of preparations for the sound film. The introduction of sound films then, for a time, brought an easing of the situation. There were two reasons for this: sound films brought the masses back to the cinema, and they also created a fresh solidarity between new capital from the electrical industry and film capital. Looked at from outside, therefore, the sound film promoted national interests; but looked at from within it made film production even more international than before.

8. This polarity is prevented from receiving due attention in the aesthetics of Idealism, which conceptually admits beauty only as something undivided (so excludes it as being divided). Nevertheless, in Hegel it makes its presence felt as clearly as can be imagined within the bounds of Idealism. 'Images,' we read in the *Lectures on the Philosophy of History*, 'had been around for a long time: piety required them early on for its devotions, but the images did not need to be *beautiful* ones; indeed, piety found these actually disturbing. In the beautiful image there is also something external present, yet in so far as this is beautiful its spirit speaks to mankind; however, a key element in those devotions is the relationship to a *thing*, since they are themselves merely an unspiritual numbing of the mind [. . .]. Beautiful art [. . .] arose in the Church

itself [. . .] even though [. . .] art had already stepped outside the *principe* of the Church.' A passage in the *Lectures on Aesthetics* also indicates that Hegel was aware of a problem here. As we read in these *Lectures*: '[. . .] We are beyond being able to venerate works of art as divine, offering them our worship; the impression they make is of a more considered kind, and what they arouse in us requires a higher touchstone.'

9. The transition from the first type of artistic reception to the second determines the historical course of artistic reception generally. Nevertheless, a certain oscillation between the two poles of reception can in principle be demonstrated for each individual work of art. Take the Sistine *Madonna*, for instance. Since Hubert Grimme's study we have known that the Sistine *Madonna* was originally painted for display purposes. Grimme was prompted to undertake his research by the question: what is the point of the wooden shelf in the foreground of the painting on which the two *putti* are leaning? How (Grimme went on to ask) did an artist like Raphael come to furnish heaven with a pair of portières? Investigation revealed that the Sistine *Madonna* had been commissioned on the occasion of the public lying-in-state of Pope Sixtus. Popes lay in state in a particular side chapel of St Peter's. At the rear of this chapel, which was shaped like a niche, Raphael's painting rested on the coffin during the lying-in-state ceremony. What Raphael shows in the painting is the Madonna emerging from the niche framed by the two green portière curtains and approaching the pope's coffin, walking on clouds. At the memorial service for Sixtus, this outstanding display value of Raphael's painting came into its own. Some time later the painting was mounted on the high altar of the abbey church of the Black Monks

in Piacenza. The reason for this exile lies in Roman ritual. Roman ritual forbids images that have been used for lying-in-state ceremonies to be used for worship at the high altar. Raphael's work was to some extent devalued by this provision. To get a proper price for it all the same, the Curia decided to include in the sale its tacit permission to use the painting on the high altar. And to avoid a row, it was arranged that the painting should go to a monastic brotherhood in a remote provincial town.

10. Similar considerations, but at a different level, are raised by Brecht: 'If the term "work of art" is no longer suitable for the thing that emerges when a work of art becomes a commodity, we must carefully and discreetly (yet without trepidation) drop the term if we do not wish simultaneously to abolish the function of that commodity, because this is a phase it must go through, and I mean that quite literally, this is no casual deviation from the correct path, what happens to it here is going to change it profoundly, eradicating its past to an extent that, were the old term to be resumed (and it will be, why not?), it will have ceased to evoke any reminder of what it once described.'

11. 'Film [. . .] supplies (or might supply): practical conclusions regarding human actions in detail [. . .]. Any kind of character-based motivation is lacking, the inner life of the characters never furnishes the main cause and is rarely the main result of the action' [Brecht]. The broadening of the field of what can be tested that the camera brings about in the screen actor matches the extraordinary broadening of the field of what can be tested that has come about for the individual as a result of economic circumstances. The importance of vocational-aptitude tests, for example, is growing all the time.

Vocational-aptitude testing is concerned with isolated bits of the individual's performance. Both filming and vocational-aptitude testing proceed before a body of experts. The director in a film studio occupies precisely the same position as the test conductor in a vocational-aptitude test.

12. Certain ostensibly minor details by which the film director distances himself from what is done in the theatre assume added interest in this context. One is the experiment of having the actor play without make-up that, among others, Dreyer conducts in his *Joan of Arc*. He spent months finding the forty or so actors who form the court of inquisition. The search for these actors resembled one for props hard to get hold of. Dreyer went to enormous lengths to avoid similarities of age, build and physiognomy. If the actor becomes a prop, the prop on the other hand not infrequently functions as an actor. Certainly there is nothing unusual about film finding itself in the position of giving a prop a part. Rather than pick at random from an infinity of examples, let us cite just one that has particular probative value. A clock that is going will always simply be an irritant onstage. Its role (measuring time) can never be assigned to it in the theatre. Even in a naturalistic play, astronomical time would conflict with stage time. So it is most significant that film, on occasion, has no trouble using a clock to measure time. This, more clearly than many other features, indicates how, under certain circumstances, every single prop is capable of assuming crucial functions. From here it is but a step to Pudowkin's assertion that 'acting associated with and based upon an object will [. . .] always be among the most powerful methods of filmic creation'. This makes film the first artistic medium capable of demonstrating

how matter acts along with man. Film can therefore constitute an outstanding tool of materialistic representation.

13. The altered mode of representation noted here as resulting from reproductive technology can also be seen in politics. Part of the crisis currently afflicting the bourgeois democracies is a crisis in the conditions influencing the representation of those who rule. The democracies place the ruler on display directly, in person, and they do it in front of MPs. Parliament is his audience! With innovations in recording equipment making the person speaking, while he is speaking, audible to and shortly afterwards visible to vast numbers, the stress is on how the politician conducts himself in front of that recording equipment. Parliaments are emptying at the same time as theatres. Radio and film are changing not only the function of the professional actor but equally the function of the person who, as rulers do, portrays himself before them. The direction of that change is the same (their different specialist tasks notwithstanding) for the screen actor as it is for the ruler. It seeks to display testable, indeed adoptable achievements in specific social conditions. This gives rise to a new kind of selection, a selection in front of the camera, from which the star and the dictator emerge as victors.

14. The privileged character of the technologies concerned is disappearing. Aldous Huxley writes:

Advances in technology have led [...] to vulgarity [...]. Process reproduction and the rotary press have made possible the indefinite multiplication of writing and pictures. Universal education and relatively high wages have created an enormous public who know how to read and can afford to buy reading and pictorial matter. A great industry has been called into existence in order to supply these commodities. Now, artistic talent is a very rare phenomenon; whence it follows [. . .] that, at every epoch and in all countries, most art has been bad. But the proportion of trash in the total artistic output is greater now than at any other period. That it must be so is a matter of simple arithmetic. The population of Western Europe has a little more than doubled during the last century. But the amount of reading – and seeing – matter has increased, I should imagine, at least twenty and possibly fifty or even a hundred times. If there were n men of talent in a population of x millions, there will presumably be $2n$ men of talent among $2x$ millions. The situation may be summed up thus. For every page of print and pictures published a century ago, twenty or perhaps even a hundred pages are published today. But for every man of talent then living, there are now only two men of talent. It may be of course that, thanks to universal education, many potential talents which in the past would have been still-born are now enabled to realize themselves. Let us assume, then, that there are now three or even four men of talent to every one of earlier times. It still remains true to say that the consumption of reading – and seeing – matter has far outstripped the natural production of gifted writers and draughtsmen. It is the same with hearing-matter. Prosperity, the gramophone and the radio have created an audience of hearers who consume an amount of hearing-matter that has increased out of all proportion to the increase of population and the consequent natural increase of talented musicians. It follows from all this that in all the arts the output of trash is both absolutely and relatively greater than it was in the past; and that it must remain greater for just so long as the world continues to consume the present inordinate quantities of reading-matter, seeing-matter and hearing-matter. (Aldous Huxley, *Beyond the Mexique Bay*)

This is not of course a forward-looking view.

15. The audacities of the cameraman do indeed invite comparison with those of the surgical operator. In a catalogue of specifically gestural tricks of technique, Luc Durtain

includes those 'that surgery calls for in connection with certain difficult operations. To exemplify this, let me take a case from ENT surgery [. . .]; I am talking about the so-called endonasal perspective procedure; or let me refer to the acrobatic tricks that, guided by the reversed image in the laryngoscope, throat surgery is obliged to perform; I might also mention aural surgery, which is reminiscent of the precision work of the watchmaker. What elaborate sequences of the most delicate muscular acrobatics are not required of the man who would repair or rescue the human body? Just think of a cataract operation, where what almost amounts to a discussion goes on between the surgeon's steel and tissue parts that are virtually fluid, or those momentous interventions in the abdominal cavity (laparotomy).'

16. This way of looking at things may seem crude; however, as that great theoretician Leonardo shows, there may be a time for consulting crude ways of looking at things. Leonardo compares painting and music like this: 'Painting is superior to music because it need not die as soon as it has received life, as is the case with poor music [. . .]. Music, which vanishes the moment after it comes into being, is no match for painting, which with the use of varnish has become eternal.'

17. If we are looking for an analogy with this situation, we shall find an instructive one in Renaissance painting. Here too we encounter an art whose unparalleled rise and importance rest not least on the fact that it includes within it a number of new sciences or at any rate fresh scientific data. It makes use of anatomy as well as perspective, mathematics, meteorology and colour theory. 'What could be more remote for us,' writes Valéry, 'than the strange pretension of a Leonardo, for whom painting was

a supreme goal and among the highest manifestations of wisdom – so much so, indeed, that in his convinced opinion it called for omniscience, and he himself did not shrink from a theoretical analysis before which men today stand in awe of its depth and detail.'

18. 'A work of art,' said André Breton, 'has value only in so far as it quivers with reflections of the future.' It is indeed the case that every mature art form stands at the point where three lines of development intersect. The fact is, technology works in the first place towards a particular art form. Before film emerged, there were those little photobooks that, when rapidly thumbed before the eye, showed a boxing match or game of tennis; there were funfair machines where a sequence of images was engendered by turning a handle. Secondly, traditional art forms try hard at certain stages in their development to generate effects that are subsequently produced with casual ease by a new art form. Before film came into its own, the Dadaists sought to bring before their audiences a type of movement that someone like Chaplin then evoked naturally. Thirdly, often inconspicuous social changes work towards a change of reception from which only the new art form benefits. Before the cinema had begun to build up a specific clientele, in the '*Kaiserpanorama*' images (already no longer still images) were viewed by an assembled audience. That audience sat around a large drum-shaped structure in which a number of stereoscopes were set: one for each viewer. Behind those stereoscopes images appeared automatically, lingered for a moment, and were then replaced by others. Similar methods had to be used by Edison when he showed the earliest filmstrips (before the screen and the projection process had been invented) to a small audience, which stared into the

apparatus in which the sequence of images unwound. Incidentally, the invention of the *Kaiserpanorama* gave particularly clear expression to a dialectics of development. Shortly before film turned the viewing of images into a collective experience, in front of the stereoscopes of these rapidly obsolete establishments image-viewing by the individual once again acquired the same power as had formerly attached to the priest's contemplation of the divine image in the *cella*.

19. The theological prototype of this immersion is the awareness of being alone with one's god. It was from this awareness that, in the great age of the bourgeoisie, freedom drew the strength to shake off the tutelage of the Church. In the age of its decline, the same awareness had to take account of the latent tendency for the forces to which the individual gives expression in his dealings with the deity to be withdrawn from the affairs of the community.

20. Film is the art form that corresponds to the heightened state of mortal peril that modern man must face. The need to expose himself to shock effects is an adaptation by man to the risks that assail him. Film corresponds to deep-rooted changes in the apparatus of perception – changes that at the level of private life are felt by every pedestrian in city traffic, at the level of history by every citizen today.

21. Much as for Dadaism, film also provides important insights as regards Cubism and Futurism. Both look like incomplete experiments on the part of art to take account of the way in which the camera has permeated reality. Unlike film, these schools performed their experiments not by exploiting the camera to portray reality artistically but almost by creating an alloy from portrayed reality

plus portrayed camera. In Cubism, the chief role was played by a sort of premonition of the camera's construction, based on optics; in Futurism by a premonition of the cinematographic effects brought out by the rapid movement of the filmstrip through the camera.

22. Here, particularly with regard to the weekly newsreel, the propaganda significance of which can scarcely be exaggerated, one technological fact stands out. *Mass reproduction particularly suits reproduction of masses*. In big festival processions, monster rallies, large-scale sporting events, and war (all of which are today paraded before the camera), the mass sees itself face to face. This process, the consequences of which need no stressing, is very closely bound up with the development of reproductive and recording technology. As a rule, mass movements present themselves more clearly to the camera than to the eye. Cadres of hundreds of thousands are best captured in bird's-eye view. And if that perspective is as accessible to the human eye as to the camera, the image that the human eye carries away from the scene is not amenable to the kind of enlargement that the recorded image undergoes. In other words, mass movements (and that includes war) represent a form of human behaviour that particularly suits the camera.

Franz Kafka:
On the Tenth Anniversary of His Death

Potemkin

The story goes: Potemkin was afflicted by severe, more or less regular fits of depression, during which no one was allowed to go near him and access to his room was most strictly barred. This affliction was not mentioned at court; people were aware, above all, that any allusion to it incurred the displeasure of Empress Catherine. One of these fits of depression on the Chancellor's part lasted for an unusually long time. Grave irregularities resulted; in the registries files piled up that the Empress demanded should be dealt with, but without Potemkin's signature this was not possible. Top civil servants were at their wits' end. One day, a minor clerk named Schuwalkin happened to enter the anteroom of the Chancellor's palace, where the members of the government were as usual standing around moaning and complaining. 'What's up, your Excellencies? How may I be of service?' the zealous Schuwalkin asked. The matter was explained to him and regret expressed that his services could not be used. 'If that's all it is, gentlemen,' Schuwalkin replied, 'give the files to me. I beg of you.' The councillors of state, having nothing to lose, let themselves be persuaded, and with the bundle of files under his arm Schuwalkin set off through galleries and along corridors to Potemkin's bedchamber. Without knocking – indeed, without pausing – he pushed down the doorhandle. The door was not locked. In the gloom Potemkin, wearing a tattered nightshirt, sat in bed biting his nails. Schuwalkin marched over to the desk, dipped the pen in the ink and, without a word, thrust it into Potemkin's hand, having first placed a document (picked up at random) on his knee. After an absent-minded glance at the intruder, Potemkin sleepily executed the first signature, then a second, and eventually all of them. With the last document safely signed, Schuwalkin left the apartment without ceremony, as he had entered it, his bundle under his arm. Returning to the anteroom, he waved the files in triumph as he entered. The councillors fell upon him, snatching papers from his hands. Breathlessly, they bent over them. No one said a word; the group stood frozen. Once again, Schuwalkin approached, once again he enquired zealously: what was the reason for the gentlemen's consternation? Then his glance too fell on the signature. Document after document was signed: Schuwalkin, Schuwalkin, Schuwalkin . . .

This story is like a messenger, heralding Kafka's work two hundred years in advance. The riddle that clouds its heart is Kafka's. The world of chancelleries and registries, of stuffy, shabby, gloomy interiors is Kafka's world. The zealous Schuwalkin, who makes light of everything and is ultimately left empty-handed, is Kafka's K. Potemkin, however, who leads a brooding existence, half asleep, neglecting his appearance, in a secluded chamber that none may enter, is an ancestor of those persons of authority who in Kafka pass their time as judges in attics or secretaries in castles and who, no matter how elevated, are invariably sunken or rather sinking figures, but may suddenly, be they the lowest-ranking dregs of the earth (doorkeepers and clerks worn out with age), appear without warning in their full panoply of power. What are they brooding about? Are they perhaps descended from those atlantes who bear the globe on their shoulders? Possibly that is why they hold their heads 'sunk so low on the breast that very little could be seen of the [. . .] eyes', like the castle governor in his portrait or Klamm when alone? But it is not the globe they bear; only the fact that even the most ordinary detail carries weight: 'His exhaustion is that of the gladiator after combat, but his work was painting a corner of a clerks' room white.' Georg Lukács once said: to make a decent table nowadays, a person must have the architectural genius of a Michelangelo. Where Lukács thought in centuries, Kafka thinks in aeons. It is for aeons that the man painting must endure. And so on, down to the least significant gesture. Many times, often for some odd reason, Kafka's figures clap their hands. Once, however, it is said in passing that those hands are 'really steam hammers'.

In steady, slow movement (sinking or ascending) we get to know these persons of authority. But nowhere are they more terrible than where they rise up out of the deepest decrepitude: out of the ancestors. To reassure the impassive, age-enfeebled father whom he has just gently put to bed, the son says: ' "Don't worry, you're well covered up." "No, I'm not!" his father shouted, slamming the answer down on the question, and he threw the quilt back with such force that for a moment it opened out completely in flight. He stood up in bed, one hand pressed lightly to the ceiling. "You wanted to cover me up, you scoundrel, I know you did, but I'm not covered up yet. If it's my last ounce of strength it's enough for you – more than enough for you. [. . .] But luckily for your father he doesn't need anyone to teach him to see through his son." [. . .] And he stood without holding on at all and kicked his legs in the air. His eyes blazed with insight. [. . .] "So now you know what else there was apart from you. [. . .] You were an innocent child, to tell the truth – though to tell the whole truth you were the devil incarnate!"' In throwing off the burden of the bedcover, the father is throwing off the weight of the world. He must set aeons in motion if he is to bring the age-old father–son relationship to life, render it fraught with consequences. But what consequences they are! He sentences the son to death by drowning. The father is the punisher. He is drawn to guilt like the officers of the court.

There is much to suggest that for Kafka the world of officialdom and the paternal world are similar. The similarity dishonours both, comprising as it does impassiveness, decrepitude and filth. The father's uniform is badly stained; his underwear is soiled. Filth is the vital element of officialdom. 'She could not understand why there was this coming and going of parties at all. "To dirty the front steps," an official had once answered her, probably in irritation, but to her that had been most enlightening [. . .].' To such an extent is uncleanness the attribute of officials that they might almost be thought of as giant parasites. Not in an economic sense, of course, but as regards the forces of good sense and humanity from which this species draws life. But so, in Kafka's peculiar families, does the father draw life from the son, squatting on him like some monstrous parasite, sucking away not only at his strength but at his right to be there. The father, the punisher, is at the same time also the prosecutor. The sin of which he accuses the son is apparently a kind of original sin. Because whom does the definition that Kafka gives of it affect more than the son? 'The original sin, the ancient wrong that man committed, consists in the reproach that man persistently levels that a wrong has been done him, that the original sin was committed against him.' But who stands accused of that original, hereditary sin (the sin of having made an heir) if not the father by the son? The sinner, in that case, would be the son. Not that we should conclude from Kafka's words that the accusation is sinful because false. Nowhere does Kafka say that it is wrongly levelled. It is a never-ending trial that is pending here, and no case can appear in a worse light than the one in which the father enlists the solidarity of this officialdom, these judicial chambers. Their boundless corruptibility is not the worst thing about them. The fact is, at heart they are so constituted that their venality offers the only hope to which humanity can cling in their regard.

The courts, of course, have access to law books. But they may not be seen. ' "[. . .] It's characteristic of this judicial system that a man is condemned not only when he's innocent but also in ignorance",' K. surmises. Laws and defined standards are still, in former times, unwritten laws. A person may overstep them unsuspectingly, thus falling into sin. But however unfortunately they affect the unsuspecting, their occurrence is not, in the sense of right, mere chance but rather fate – here showing itself in its ambiguous aspect. In a brief consideration of the old idea of fate, Hermann Cohen says it is an 'insight that becomes inescapable' that it is its 'dispositions themselves that appear to prompt and bring about this emergence, this apostasy'. It is the same with the jurisdiction whose proceedings are directed against K. This goes back long before the era of the Law of the Twelve Tables into a primordial world that saw one of the first victories of written law. Here, the law may be written down in law books but it is still secret, and on this basis the primordial world exercises its dominion with all the less restraint.

Circumstances in official and family life touch in many different ways in Kafka. In the village under Castle Hill they have an expression that sheds some light here. ' "There's a saying here, perhaps you know it: 'Official decisions have the shyness of young girls.' " "That's a good observation," K. said [. . .], "a good observation, the decisions may also have other properties in common with girls." ' The most remarkable thing about them is that they lend themselves to everything, like the shy young girls who meet K. in *The Castle* and *The Trial* and who give themselves over to fornication in the bosom of the family as in a bed. He comes across them at every step of the way; the rest follows as casually as the conquest of the barmaid. '[. . .] They embraced, the little body burning in K.'s hands, in a state of oblivion from which K. tried repeatedly yet vainly to extricate himself they rolled several steps, thudding into Klamm's door, then lay in the little puddles of beer and the rest of the rubbish covering the floor. There hours passed [. . .] in which K. constantly had the feeling he had lost his way or wandered farther into a strange land than anyone before him, a strange land where even the air held no trace of the air at home, where a man must suffocate from the strangeness yet into whose foolish enticements he could do nothing but plunge on, getting even more lost.' We shall hear more about this strangeness later. What is remarkable, though, is that these whorish women are never seen as beautiful. Instead, beauty in Kafka's world crops up only in the most secret places: among defendants, for instance. 'In fact, this is a remarkable, almost a scientific, phenomenon [. . .]. It can't be guilt making them handsome [. . .]; nor can it be the right punishment beautifying them in advance [. . .], so it must have something to do with the proceedings instituted against them rubbing off on them in some way.'

One gathers from *The Trial* that those proceedings are usually hopeless so far as the defendants are concerned – even where acquittal remains a hope for them. It may be that very hopelessness that makes them the only characters in Kafka to exhibit beauty. At least that would chime very well with a fragment of conversation handed down by Max Brod. 'I recall [he writes] one conversation with Kafka that began with present-day Europe and the decline of humankind. "We," he said, "are nihilistic thoughts, suicidal reflections arising in God's mind." At first this made me think of the Gnostic world view:

God as evil demiurge, the world as his Fall. "Oh no," he said, "our world is only a bad mood on God's part, like having a bad day." "So there'd be hope, then, outside this phenomenon we know as world?" He smiled: "Oh, there's hope enough, an infinity of hope – only not for us."' The words form a link to those most curious of Kafka's figures who are the only ones to have escaped the bosom of the family and for whom there is possibly hope. They are not the animals, not even the cross-breeds or fantasy beings such as the cat-lamb or Odradek. All these do still live under the spell of the family. Not for nothing does Gregory Samsa wake up as a bug right in the parental home, not for nothing is the peculiar animal that is half cat and half lamb an heirloom handed down on the paternal side, not for nothing is Odradek 'The Householder's Concern'. The 'assistants', however, do indeed fall outside this circle.

These assistants belong to a group of figures that permeate Kafka's entire work. They include not only the confidence trickster who is unmasked in 'Looking to See' but also the student seen on the balcony at night as Karl Rossmann's neighbour as well as the fools who live in that city in the south and 'don't get tired'. The twilight that shrouds their existence recalls the wavering light in which the playlets of Robert Walser (author of the novel *The Apprentice*, which Kafka adored) have their characters appear. Indian sagas tell of the Gandharvas, incomplete creatures, beings at the hazy stage. Kafka's assistants are of that kind; not belonging to any of the other groups of figures but no strangers to them either; the messengers toing and froing between them. They look, Kafka informs us, like Barnabas, and he is a messenger. They are not yet quite free of the lap of Mother Nature, which is why they have 'installed themselves on the floor in a corner, using two old dresses, it was their ambition [. . .] to take up as little room as possible, to this end they tried various methods, always of course with much whispering and giggling, they crossed their arms and legs, they crouched down, the two of them, at dawn and dusk all that could be seen in their corner was one big huddle'. For them and their kind, the immature and inept, hope still exists.

What is discernible as tenderly non-committal about the way these messengers are is in an oppressive, sombre fashion law as regards this whole world of creatures. None has its fixed position, its fixed, unexchangeable outline; none that is not in the process of rising or falling; none that does not swap places with its enemy or its neighbours; none that has not completed its time yet is immature, none that is not profoundly exhausted yet is only at the beginning of a long haul. All talk of orders and hierarchies is impossible here. The world of myth that this suggests is incomparably younger than Kafka's world, to which myth itself promised redemption. But if we know one thing, it is this: that Kafka did not take its lure. A latter-day Odysseus, he let it slide away from 'eyes fixed on the distance, the Sirens literally vanished away in the face of his determination, and precisely when he was closest to them he was no longer aware of them at all'. Among the forebears that Kafka has in the Ancient World, the Jewish ones and the Chinese ones that we shall come across later, this Greek one must not be overlooked. The fact is, Odysseus stands on the threshold separating myth and fairy tale. Trickery has slipped reason and cunning into myth; no longer are the powers of myth invincible. Fairy tales are a handing-down of this victory over them. And fairy tales for dialecticians are what Kafka wrote when he embarked on legends. He inserted little tricks into them; then he read from them evidence 'that even inadequate means, indeed childish means can bring salvation'. It is with these words that he begins his story, 'The Sirens' Silence'. With him, the Sirens do in fact employ silence; they possess 'an even more frightful weapon than song – namely, their silence'. They used it against Odysseus. He, however, Kafka tells us, 'was so full of cunning, he was such a fox, that not even the goddess of fate could penetrate his inmost being. Possibly, although this passes human understanding, he really had noted the Sirens' silence and to parry them and the gods had held up this sham,' as he relates, 'merely as a sort of shield.'

With Kafka, the Sirens are silent. Maybe, too, because with him music and song are an expression or at least a pledge of escape. A pledge of hope, which we have from that small, simultaneously immature and everyday, simultaneously comforting and foolish intermediate world in which the assistants are at home. Kafka is like the lad who set out to learn how to be afraid. He stumbled upon Potemkin's palace but ultimately, in the cellars of that palace, upon Josephine, the singing mouse whose manner Kafka describes like this: 'Something of our poor, short-lived childhood is there, something of a lost happiness we shall never see again, but also some-

thing of our busy present existence and its small, unfathomable yet persistent and quite inextinguishable element
of gaiety.'

A childhood picture

There is a picture of Kafka as a child, rarely has this
'poor, short-lived childhood' left a more touching image.
It was doubtless taken in one of those nineteenth-century
studios that with their drapes and palms, tapestries and
easels occupy so equivocal a place between torture-
chamber and throne-room. There, in a tight-fitting,
somehow humiliating child's outfit overloaded with lace
trimmings stands the approximately six-year-old boy in
a sort of conservatory landscape. Palm fronds stand stiffly
in the background. And as if to make this upholstered
version of the tropics even more suffocating and sultry,
the model holds in his left hand a disproportionately
large, broad-brimmed hat of the kind Spaniards have. An
immeasurably sad gaze commands the landscape set out
before it, into which the shell of one large ear listens
intently.

Ardent 'Wanting to be a Red Indian' may once have
consumed this great grief: 'Ah, if one were a Red Indian,
on the alert immediately, and if leaning into the wind
on one's galloping horse one went quivering swiftly over
the quavering ground, over and over again till one stopped
using the spurs, there being no spurs, till one threw away
the reins, there being no reins, and one scarcely saw the
terrain out in front as a well-mown stretch of moorland

without even a horse's neck now and a horse's head.'
Much is contained in that wish. Fulfilment betrays its
secret. This it finds in America. The fact that there is
something special behind *America* emerges from the
hero's name. While in the earlier novels [after Benjamin
wrote this it became clear that *America* was in fact the
first of Kafka's novels] the author never addressed himself
otherwise than with the murmured initial, here he is
reborn with a full name on a new continent. He experiences that rebirth in the Oklahoma Nature Theatre. 'Karl
saw a poster on a street corner, bearing the following
inscription: Today, on the Clayton Racetrack, from six
in the morning till midnight, staff will be taken on for
the Oklahoma Theatre! The great Theatre of Oklahoma
is calling you! It will call only today, only the once!
Anyone missing the chance now misses it for ever!
Anyone thinking of his future is one of us! All are
welcome! Anyone wishing to become an artiste, sign up
now! We are the theatre that can use everyone, each in
his place! Whoever has plumped for us, congratulations
right now! But hurry if you want to be admitted by
midnight! At twelve everything closes, never to reopen.
Be damned, anyone who disbelieves us! To Clayton, one
and all!' The person reading this announcement is Karl
Rossmann ['horseman'], the third and more fortunate
incarnation of K., who is the hero of Kafka's novels.
Happiness awaits him at the Oklahoma Nature Theatre,
which is an actual racetrack, as 'unhappiness' [in the
story so entitled] had once overwhelmed him as he
'began pacing the narrow carpet in my room as if it had
been a racetrack'. Ever since Kafka had written 'For

Jockeys to Ponder' and had 'The new attorney' '[. . .] hoisting his legs up high [. . .] with each footfall ringing out on the marble' stride up the courthouse steps and his 'Children in the lane' go trotting into the country, arms linked, taking great leaps, this is a figure he had come to know well, and it is indeed possible for Karl Rossmann, 'distracted as a result of his sleepiness, [to make] frequent excessively high, time-consuming, pointless leaps'. So it can only be on a racetrack that he attains the goal of his desires.

That racetrack is at the same time a theatre, which gives rise to a riddle. However, the enigmatic location and the wholly un-enigmatic, thoroughly transparent and straightforward figure of Karl Rossmann belong together. Karl Rossmann, in fact, is transparent, straightforward, almost characterless in the sense in which Franz Rosenzweig says in *The Star of Redemption* that in China the inner person is 'almost characterless; the concept of the wise man, as classically [. . .] embodied in Kung-fu-tzu [Confucius], disregards any possibility of distinctiveness of character; he is the truly characterless man – the average man, in fact [. . .]. It is something quite other than character that distinguishes the Chinese individual: a wholly elemental purity of feeling.' No matter how it is communicated intellectually (it may be that this purity of feeling is a particularly sensitive balance weighing gestural behaviour), in any case the Oklahoma Nature Theatre refers back to Chinese theatre, which is indeed a gestural theatre. Among the most important functions of that Nature Theatre is to dissolve events into gesture. One might, indeed, go further and say:

quite a number of Kafka's smaller studies and stories
only appear in their full light when translated, as it were,
into acts in the Oklahoma Nature Theatre. Only then will
it be seen for certain that Kafka's entire work represents a
codex of gestures that do not, in and of themselves,
possess any fixed symbolic meaning for the author;
instead, in constantly changing contexts and ever-
different experimental arrangements, they are asked to
furnish such meaning. The theatre is the proper place
for such experimental arrangements. In an unpublished
commentary on the story 'A Case of Fratricide', Werner
Kraft perceptively sees the unfolding of this little tale in
dramatic terms. 'The play can begin, and it really is
announced by the ringing of a bell. This happens in the
most natural way in that Wese leaves the building in
which his office is situated. However, this doorbell (we
are told explicitly) rings "too loudly for a doorbell, out
over the city, upwards at the sky".' As that bell, which
makes too much noise for a doorbell, rings up at the sky,
so the gesturing of Kafka's figures is too intrusive for the
normal environment, breaking into one more spacious.
The more Kafka's mastery increased, the less often he
bothered to match those gestures to everyday situations,
to explain them. '"Funny habit, that,"' we read in 'The
Metamorphosis', '"his sitting on the desk and talking
down to his employees from a great height, especially
since you have to step right up close because of his
deafness."' Such giving of reasons had already been left
far behind in *The Trial* [in the penultimate chapter of
which we read that K.]: 'stopped by the first row of pews,
but the distance still seemed too great for the priest, who

stretched out his hand and pointed with a sharply bent
finger to a spot right in front of the pulpit. K. followed
this instruction too. From this spot he had to bend his
head far back to keep the priest in view.'

When Max Brod says, 'It was unpredictable, the world
of the things that mattered to him,' the thing that was
least predictable so far as Kafka was concerned was
gesture. Each gesture constitutes a process, one might
almost say a drama, of its own. The stage on which that
drama plays out is the world theatre, whose backdrop is
the sky. On the other hand that sky is nothing more than
a backdrop; studying it on its own terms would mean
putting a frame round the piece of painted cloth and
hanging it in a gallery. Kafka, like El Greco, tears open
the sky behind each gesture; but, as in El Greco (who
was the patron saint of the Expressionists), the decisive
thing, the centre of the event, is gesture. They are bowed
with alarm as they emerge, the people who had heard
the 'knock on the courtyard gate'. That is how a Chinese
actor would portray alarm, not how someone would
react to being startled. Elsewhere K. himself puts on an
act: with semi-unconscious deliberation, 'slowly [. . .]
turning his eyes up cautiously [. . .] he picked up one
of the papers from the desk without looking, placed it
on the palm of his hand and gradually raised it to the
level of the two men as he himself got to his feet. He
had no definite thought in mind as he was doing this but
acted only because he felt this was how he must conduct
himself once he had completed the great plea which
was to relieve him completely of anxiety.' Maximum
strangeness coupled with maximum simplicity marks

this gesture out as animal. It is possible to read quite a long way into Kafka's animal stories without realizing for one moment that these are not people. If one then comes across the name of the creature (monkey, dog or mole), one looks up in alarm to see that one is already a long way from the continent of man. Kafka, however, is that all the time; he robs human gesture of its traditional props and then possesses, in it, an object prompting unending reflections.

But they are also, oddly, never-ending when they proceed from Kafka's epigrammatic stories. Think of the parable 'At the Door of the Law'. Coming across this in *A Country Doctor*, the reader may possibly have been struck by the cloudy place deep within it. But would he have embarked on the apparently endless series of thoughts that spring from this parable at the point where Kafka sets out to interpret it? This happens through the priest in *The Trial* – and it happens at so marked a place that one might suppose the novel to be simply the parable unfolded. But the word 'unfolded' carries two meanings. The bud unfolds to become a flower, but so does the little boat that one teaches children to make unfold to become a flat sheet of paper. And it is this second type of 'unfolding' that actually suits parables, the reader's pleasure lying in smoothing the parable out in such a way that its meaning becomes plain. Kafka's parables, though, unfold in the first sense; they unfold as the bud becomes flower. Their product, therefore, is not unlike poetry. That does not prevent his pieces from not fitting entirely into the prose forms of the West and occupying a position, as regards doctrine, similar to that of Haggadah over against Halacha. They are not allegories, yet nor do they want to be taken straight; they are so constituted that they can be quoted and told by way of explanation. But are we in possession of the doctrine that Kafka's allegories accompany and that is explained in K.'s gestures and in how his animals conduct themselves physically? It is not there; at most, we can say that this and that allude to it. Kafka might have said: hand it down as its relic; we, however, can equally say: prepares it as its forerunner. In either case, the question at issue is the organization of life and work in the human community. This preoccupied Kafka with mounting constancy, the less comprehensible it became to him. Where Napoleon, in the famous 'Erfurt Conversation' with Goethe, put politics in place of fate, Kafka (in a variant of this dictum) might have defined organization as destiny. And it is not only in the extensive official hierarchies of *The Trial* and *The Castle* that he sees organization but also, even more tangibly, in the difficulties and immensities of a building project, the venerable model of which he wrote about in 'Building the Great Wall of China'.

The wall was designed to provide protection for the centuries; so the most careful construction, drawing upon the architectural expertise of all known eras and nations, and a constant sense of personal responsibility on the part of those doing the building were essential prerequisites for the job. For humbler tasks, of course, it was possible to use ignorant day labourers from among the people, men, women, children, anyone available for good money; but to be in charge of even four day labourers called for someone sensible, trained in building work

[. . .]. We (I am probably speaking for many people here) found that it was only through actually spelling out the orders of top management that we came to know ourselves and made the discovery that, without management, neither our book-learning nor our common sense would have sufficed for the tiny office that we fulfilled within the wider whole.

Such organization is not unlike fate. Metchnikoff, who in his famous book *Civilization and the Great Historical Rivers* outlined the subject, does so in phrases that might be from Kafka.

The canals of the Yangtse-kiang and the dams of the Hoang-ho are in all probability a result of skilfully organized collective work on the part of [. . .] generations [. . .]. The slightest inadvertency in cutting this or that trench or in supporting some dam or other, the least bit of carelessness, a piece of selfish behaviour on the part of a person or group of people in the matter of preserving the joint water resource, will in such unusual circumstances become the source of some social ill and widespread collective misfortune. Accordingly, a tributary will under threat of death demand close and enduring solidarity among masses of the population that are in many instances strangers to one another, even enemies; it sentences Everyman to tasks whose common usefulness becomes apparent only with time and whose overall plan very often far exceeds the understanding of the ordinary person.

Kafka wanted to know that he was accounted an ordinary person. The limit of understanding having constricted his every step, he is keen to constrict others likewise.

Sometimes he seems close to Dostoevsky's Grand Inquisitor in saying [in effect]: 'We thus face a mystery we cannot grasp. And the very fact that it is a riddle gave us the right to preach it, to teach people that what matters is not freedom, not love, but the riddle, the secret, the mystery to which they must place themselves in thrall – unthinkingly, even in defiance of conscience.' The temptations of mysticism are something that Kafka did not always avoid. Concerning his encounter with Rudolf Steiner we have a diary entry that does not, at least in its published form, embody Kafka's view. Was he being evasive here? The way in which he treated his own texts makes this seem by no means impossible. Kafka had a rare strength when it came to keeping himself supplied with allegories. Even so, he never pours his all into what can be deciphered; on the contrary, he took every conceivable precaution against having his texts interpreted. Circumspectly, meticulously, mistrustfully we must grope our way forward into their heart. We need to bear in mind Kafka's peculiar way of reading as applied to interpreting the said parables. We are also permitted to recall his last will and testament. His injunction to destroy a legacy is on closer examination as hard to understand and calls for the same meticulous consideration as the answers given by the doorkeeper 'At the Door of the Law'. Possibly Kafka, whom every day of his existence confronted with impenetrable modes of behaviour and announcements that were not clear, wanted in death at least to pay back his fellows in the same coin.

Kafka's world is a world theatre. For him, man is in

and of himself onstage, the proof being that everyone is taken on at the Oklahoma Nature Theatre. The criteria governing such admission are unfathomable. A talent for playacting, one immediately supposes, but apparently that is irrelevant. However, another way of putting it is: candidates are given no other task than that of playing themselves. That they may, when it comes down to it, actually *be* the person they are acting lies outside the realm of possibility. It is through their roles that such characters seek a place in the Nature Theatre, as Pirandello's six are in search of an author. For both groups, this is the place of ultimate refuge; and that does not exclude its constituting redemption. Redemption is not a reward for existence; it is the last excuse of someone of whom Kafka says that 'his own browbone blocks his path'. And the law of this theatre is implicit in a sentence tucked away in 'A Report for an Academy': 'I [imitated men] because I was in search of a way out and for no other reason.' For K. a glimmering of these things seems to arise before the end of his trial. He turns abruptly to the two men in top hats who have come to take him away and asks: '"At what theatre are you playing?" "Theatre?" enquired one gentleman of the other, the corners of his mouth twitching. The other gestured like a mute struggling with an unmanageable animal.' They leave the question unanswered, but several things point to its having had an effect on them.

At a long bench covered with a white cloth all who are henceforth at the Nature Theatre are served. 'Everyone was happy and excited.' Extras block in the moves for angels to mark the occasion. They stand on tall pedestals that, covered with billowing robes, have flights of stairs inside them. The trappings of a country fair, maybe of a children's party, too, where the tightly laced-up, scrubbed-up boy we were talking about earlier possibly lost his sad look. But for their tied-on wings, these angels could be real. They have their precursors in Kafka. The manager is one of them, stepping up on the seat to reach the trapeze artist where he lies in the luggage rack afflicted by his 'First Sorrow' and stroking him and pressing the trapeze artist's face to his own 'so that he too was bathed in the trapeze artist's tears'. Another, a guardian angel or simply a 'guardian of the law', takes care of the murderer Schmar after the 'Case of Fratricide', the same Schmar as has 'his lips pressed to the shoulder of the policeman who nimbly leads him away'. In Oklahoma's rural ceremonies Kafka's last novel dies away. 'Kafka's work,' writes Soma Morgenstern, 'has the whiff of village air about it, as is the case with all great founders of religion.' Here we are the more entitled to recall Lao-tzu's portrayal of piety for the fact that Kafka provided the most perfect description of it in 'The Next Village'. Lao-tzu wrote: 'Neighbouring lands may lie within sight, / We may hear one another's cocks crowing, one another's dogs barking; / Yet folk should die at a ripe old age / Without having travelled there and back.' Kafka also wrote parables, but he did not found a religion.

Let us consider the village lying at the foot of Castle Hill from which K.'s alleged summons as a land surveyor is so puzzlingly and surprisingly confirmed. In his afterword to this novel Brod mentioned that in connection with this village at the foot of Castle Hill Kafka had a particular place in mind, Zürau in the Erz Mountains. We, however, may be permitted to recognize it as a different village. It is the one in a Talmudic legend related by the rabbi when someone asks him why Jews prepare a festive meal on Friday evenings. It tells of a princess who, in exile, far from her compatriots, living in a village where she does not understand the language, finds herself languishing. One day the princess receives a letter: her betrothed has not forgotten her, he has set out, he is on his way to her. The betrothed, explains the rabbi, is the Messiah, the princess is the soul, but the village to which she has been exiled is the body. And being unable to tell the village (which does not know her language) of her joy in any other way, she prepares a meal for it. With that village in the Talmud, we are in the midst of Kafka's world. Because just like K. in the village below Castle Hill, present-day man lives in his body; his body eludes him, it is an alien presence. One day a person may wake up to find himself transformed into a verminous bug. What is alien (alien to him) is now his lord and master. The air of this village blows through Kafka's work, which is why he was not tempted to found a religion. The same village contains the pigsty from which the horses emerge for the country doctor, the stuffy back room in which Klamm, cigar in mouth, sits in front of a glass of beer, and the courtyard door, knocking on which brings in the end. The air in this village is neither pure nor free from all the not-yet-become and already overripe things that form a putrid blend. Kafka was obliged to breathe it all his life. He was neither soothsayer nor founder of a religion. How did he survive in it?

The hunchback dwarf

Knut Hamsun, we learned a while ago, was in the habit of occasionally giving the letters column of the local paper in the little town near which he lived the benefit of his views. In that town, some years back, a jury was trying a girl who had killed her newborn child. She was sentenced to a term in jail. Shortly afterwards, Hamsun voiced his opinion in the local paper. He announced that he would be turning his back on a town that gave a mother who murdered her baby anything but the maximum sentence; if not the gallows, then imprisonment for life. Several years passed. [Hamsun's] *Growth of the Soil* came out, containing the story of a serving-girl who commits the same crime, receives the same sentence, and, as the reader can clearly see, had undoubtedly not deserved a heavier one.

Kafka's thoughts as handed down in 'Building the Great Wall of China' prompt us to recall this sequence of events. Because hardly had this posthumous volume appeared than, on the basis of those thoughts, a reading of Kafka began to prevail that enjoyed interpreting the thoughts and took correspondingly little notice of Kafka's actual writings. There are two ways of fundamentally missing the point of Kafka's work. The natural interpretation is one, the supernatural the other; in essence, both interpretations (the psychoanalytical and the theological) shoot past the target in similar ways. The first is represented by Hellmuth Kaiser; the second by quite a few authors already – H. J. Shoeps, Bernhard Rang and

Groethuysen among them. Their number also includes Willy Haas, who in other contexts (we shall come across these later) has of course said some revealing things about Kafka. These insights were not able to keep him from laying a kind of theological grid over Kafka's work as a whole. 'The supreme power,' he writes of Kafka, 'the realm of grace, was portrayed by him in his great novel *The Castle*, the lower realm, that of judgement and damnation, in his equally great novel *The Trial*. The world between the two [. . .], our earthly fate and its difficult demands, he sought to reproduce in severely stylized form in a third novel, *America*.' The first third of this interpretation can probably, since Brod, be seen as the common property of Kafka interpretation. In this sense Bernhard Rang, for instance, writes: 'In so far as the Castle may be seen as the seat of grace, the meaning in theological terms of all this vain striving and seeking is that God's grace cannot be arbitrarily and deliberately invoked and coerced by man. Restlessness and impatience will be baffled and bewildered only by the solemn stillness of the divine.' It is a comfortable reading; that it is also an untenable one becomes increasingly clear, the further it ventures. Possibly, therefore, with the greatest clarity in Willi Haas, when he states: 'Kafka comes [. . .] from Kierkegaard as well as from Pascal, in fact he can be called the sole legitimate grandchild of Kierkegaard and Pascal. All three are basically driven by the harsh, utterly harsh religious motive: that man is always in the wrong before God.' Kafka's 'higher world, his so-called "Castle" with its unpredictable, pettifogging, thoroughly lubricious staff, his curious heaven is playing a ghastly game with mankind [. . .]; yet man is very deeply in the wrong even before this God.' This theology falls well behind the justification doctrine of Anselm of Canterbury in terms of barbaric speculations – which incidentally do not even seem reconcilable with the way Kafka's text is worded. 'I mean,' we read in *The Castle*, 'can an individual official grant a pardon? At best, that might be a matter for the authority as a whole, though even it can probably not grant a pardon, only issue a directive.' The path thus taken quickly petered out. 'All that,' says Denis de Rougement, 'is not the wretched condition of mankind without God but the actual wretchedness of mankind stuck with a God he does not know, not knowing Christ.'

It is easier to draw speculative conclusions from the collection of notes left by Kafka than to fathom even one of the motives that appear in his stories and novels. However, only they will supply some explanation of the primeval forces that harnessed and rode Kafka's work; forces that can of course also, and with equal justification, be seen as secular forces in today's world. And who is to say under what name they appeared to Kafka himself? Only this much is certain: placed among them, he did not find his way home. He did not know them. All he could see, in the mirror that held up the primeval world in front of him in the form of guilt, was the future as courtroom. But how is one to take this – is this not the Last Judgement? Does it not turn judge into defendant? Are not the proceedings now the sentence? To these questions, Kafka gave no answer. Did he have hopes in this direction? Or was it not like that at all, was he actually more concerned with postponing the sentence? In the stories we have of his, epic poetry means once more what it meant to Scheherazade: putting off what is to come. Postponement is what the defendant hopes for in *The Trial* – if only the proceedings did not gradually give way to the verdict. The Patriarch himself stands to benefit from postponement, even if he has to give up his place in the tradition in return. 'I could imagine a different Abraham, who (he wouldn't become a patriarch, of course, he wouldn't even make it to old-clothes seller) though instantly ready, with the willingness of a waiter, to perform the sacrifice demanded, did not in fact get it performed because he cannot leave home, he's indispensable, the household needs him, there's always something to be done, the house is not finished, but until his house is finished, until he has this support behind him, he can't get away, even the Bible accepts this, saying: "He prepared his house."'

'With the willingness of a waiter' this Abraham appears. There was always something that was comprehensible to Kafka only in the form of gesture. And the gesture he failed to understand forms the hazy spot in the parables. This is where Kafka's writing proceeds from. We know how he kept it to himself. His last will and testament consigns it to destruction. That document, which no study of Kafka can avoid, states that it did not satisfy its author; that he regarded his efforts as failures; that he counted himself among those who must inevitably fail. What failed was his splendid attempt to carry writing into doctrine and, as parable, restore to it the tenability and inconspicuousness that in the light of reason he saw as the only properties befitting it. No writer so precisely obeyed the commandment: 'You shall not make for yourself an idol.'

'It was as if the shame should outlive him' – these are the words that end *The Trial*. Shame, corresponding to his 'elementary purity of feeling', is Kafka's most powerful gesture. But it has two faces. Shame is an intimate reaction on the part of the individual; at the same time it is a socially discriminating one. Shame is not only shame in the presence of others; it may also be shame on their behalf. Thus Kafka's shame is no more personal than the life and thinking that it governs and of which he said: 'He does not live on account of his personal life, he does not think on account of his personal thinking. For him it is as if he lives and thinks at the urging of a family [. . .]. It is because of this unknown family [. . .] that he cannot be released.' We do not know how this unknown family (of people and animals) is made up. All that is clear is that this is what compels Kafka to move aeons in writing. At the behest of this family he trundles the rock of what has happened in history as Sisyphus rolled the boulder. What happens in the process is that the underside of the rock is exposed. It is not a pleasant sight. Kafka, however, is able to bear that sight. 'Having faith in progress does not mean believing that progress has already occurred. That would not be faith.' The age in which Kafka lives does not, for him, signify progress over against the beginnings of time. His novels play out in a swamp. The created world seems to him to be at a stage that Bachofen called 'hetaerean'. That this stage has passed into oblivion is not to say it does not extend into the present. On the contrary: it is present as a result of having passed into oblivion. An experience that goes deeper than that of the average person will come up against it. 'I have experience,' runs one of Kafka's earliest jottings, 'and I am not joking when I say it is a kind of sea-sickness on dry land.' Not for nothing is the first 'Meditation' made on a swing. And Kafka is tireless in expounding the fluctuating nature of experience. Every experience has 'give'; every experience blends with its opposite. 'It was in summer,' we read at the beginning of 'The Knock on the Courtyard Gate', 'a warm day. I and my sister, on our way home, passed a courtyard gate. I forget: was it through high spirits or in a mood of absent-mindedness that she hit the gate or did she simply shake her fist at it without aiming a blow?' The mere possibility of the turn of events mentioned in third place makes the first two, which had at first seemed innocuous, appear in a different light. It is from the soggy ground of such experiences that Kafka's female characters arise. They are swamp creatures – like Leni, who 'splayed the middle and ring fingers of her right hand apart, and the connecting membrane between them almost came up to the topmost joint of the short fingers'. 'Marvellous times,' says the ambiguous Frieda, recalling her earlier life, 'you've never asked me about my past.' The fact is, this leads into the murky depths, site of that coupling whose 'ungoverned luxuriance [as Bachofen put it] is hated by the pure powers of heavenly light and justifies the description *luteae voluptates* used by Arnobius'.

From this standpoint Kafka's narrative technique becomes comprehensible. When other characters in the novels have something to say to K., they do so (regardless of how important it is or how surprising) in a casual, incidental way, as if basically he must have known this all along. It is as if there was nothing new here, as if the hero was being asked quite unobtrusively to allow himself to recall something he had forgotten. It is in this sense that Willi Haas, trying to make sense of what happens in *The Trial*, rightly states 'that the object of these proceedings, indeed the real hero of this incredible book, is forgetting [. . .], the chief property of which is of course that it forgets itself [. . .]. It has itself become almost a mute character here in the figure of the defend-ant – a character, in fact, of the most splendid intensity.' That this 'mysterious centre' derives from 'the Jewish religion' is surely not to be dismissed out of hand. 'Here memory as piety plays a most mysterious role. It is [. . .] not *a* but in fact *the* most profound quality of Jehovah that he remembers, that he retains an infallible memory "into the third and fourth generation", indeed into the "hundredth"; the most sacred [. . .] act of [. . .] our rite is the expunging of sins from the Book of Memory.'

What is forgotten (and this discovery brings us to another threshold of Kafka's work) is never a purely individual entity. Each thing forgotten blends into the oblivion of prehistory, entering with it into innumerable, uncertain, shifting connections with more and more monstrosities. Oblivion is the vessel out of which the inexhaustible intermediate world in Kafka's stories thrusts towards the light. 'There, it is precisely the world's abundance that constitutes the sole reality. All that is spirit must have material substance, must be

distinct, to have room here and the right to exist [. . .].
The spiritual, in so far as it still plays a role, becomes
spirits. The spirits become wholly individual individuals,
each bearing its own name and having a quite specific
connection with the name of the worshipper [. . .].
Prompting no misgivings, their abundance further over-
brims the world's abundance [. . .]. Causing no concern,
the crush of spirits here increases; [. . .] more and more
new ones joining the old, each with its own name, each
distinct from all the rest.' We are not of course talking
about Kafka's world here – this is about China, and it
is how Franz Rosenzweig, in *The Star of Redemption*,
describes Chinese ancestor worship.

For Kafka, however, the immeasurability of the world
of the facts that mattered to him was matched by that of
the world of his forebears, and undoubtedly that world,
like the totem poles of primitive tribes, led down to
animals. Incidentally, it is not only in Kafka that animals
are vessels of oblivion. In Tieck's profound 'Fair Eckbert'
a forgotten dog's name (Strohmian) symbolizes an enigmatic guilt. Understandably, therefore, Kafka never tired
of trying to learn by listening to animals things that had
been forgotten. Animals are not the target, of course
not; yet without them it cannot be done. Think of the
'Fasting Artist' who, 'when all was said and done, [. . .]
was no more than an obstacle on the way to the stables'.
Do we not see the animals in 'The Burrow' and 'The
Giant Mole' mulling things over as we see them rooting
around? Even so, on the other side of that thinking there
is something highly unfocused. Such an animal will
swing indecisively from one worry to the next, giving a

nip at each fear in turn, displaying the fickleness of despair. There are butterflies, too, in Kafka; the guilt-laden 'Hunter Gracchus', who refuses to acknowledge his guilt, '[. . .] has become a butterfly. Don't laugh,' he urges. This much is certain: of all Kafka's creations it is mainly the animals that become thinkers. What corruption is to the law, fear is to their thinking. It messes up the way things go, yet it is the only hopeful thing about that way. However, since the most forgotten other is our body, our own body, we understand why Kafka called the cough that broke out of him 'the animal'. It was the extreme vanguard, the most forward position of the great herd.

The oddest bastard that, in Kafka, the primeval world procreated with guilt is Odradek. 'It looks at first glance like a flat, star-shaped spool; it even appears to be wound with thread, or rather with a lot of old odds and ends of threads knotted together, some of them tangled together, and comprising a great variety of types and colours. But it is not just a spool, because projecting from the centre of the star is a little rod forming a cross-piece, with another little rod extending from it at right angles. By means of this latter rod on one side and one of the rays of the star on the other side, the whole structure is able to stand upright as if on two legs.' Odradek 'stays by turns in the attic, on the stairs, in the corridors and in the hall'. In other words, it prefers the same places as the court investigating guilt. Floors are the site of discarded, forgotten effects. Maybe the compulsion to appear before the court evokes a similar feeling to that of going up to holes in the floor that have been sealed off for years. One would gladly postpone the enterprise until the end of time, as K. finds preparing his defence a suitable activity for 'a mind become childlike some day after retirement'.

Odradek is the form things assume in oblivion. They are distorted, all distorted, like [the object of] 'The Householder's Concern' where no one knows what it is, like the 'giant bug', which we are only too well aware represents Gregory Samsa, like the large animal, half lamb, half pussy cat, for which 'the butcher's knife [might constitute] release'. However, these figures of Kafka's are connected through a whole series of characters to the archetype of distortion, the hunchback. Among the gestures portrayed in Kafka's stories, none crops up more frequently than that of the man with his head bowed low over his chest. The cause is weariness in connection with judicial authorities, noise in connection with hotel porters, the low ceiling in connection with mine visitors. In 'In the Penal Colony', on the other hand, the authorities use an old-fashioned piece of machinery to engrave elaborate lettering on the backs of those who have been found guilty, multiplying the pricks and piling on the ornamentation until such time as the individual convict's back becomes clairvoyant and can decipher the writing itself, from the letters of which he must deduce the name of his unknown crime. It is up to the back, then. And for Kafka it has always been up to the back. An early diary entry reads: 'To be as heavy as possible, which I regard as good for getting to sleep, I had folded my arms and laid my hands on my shoulders, so that I lay there like a soldier carrying full gear.' Obviously, being loaded up goes together (for the sleeper) with forgetting, with reaching oblivion. In 'The Hunchback Dwarf', the same thing is symbolized in folksong. It is this dwarf who inhabits distorted life; he will vanish when the Messiah comes, on the subject of whom one great rabbi said that he does not wish to change the world by force but will only rearrange it slightly.

'I go to my room, / Keen to say my prayers; / There I find a hunchback dwarf / Who starts to laugh.' It is Odradek's laugh, which we are told 'sounds something like the rustle of fallen leaves'. 'As I kneel at my stool / To say a small prayer, / There I find a hunchback dwarf / Who starts to speak: / Darling child, oh please, oh please, / Say one for the hunchback dwarf!' That is how the folksong ends. In its profundity Kafka finds contact with the ground that neither 'mythical foreknowledge' nor 'existential theology' provide him with. It is the ground of German popular culture as much as Jewish. If Kafka did not pray (and we don't know), he was at least a supreme practitioner of what Malebranche calls 'the natural prayer of the mind' – attentiveness. And in it, like the saints in their prayers, he included all created being.

Sancho Panza

In a Hassidic village, so the story goes, one evening at the end of Sabbath, the Jews were sitting in a shabby inn. They were locals – all except for one, whom none of them knew, an extremely shabbily dressed, ragged person huddled in a dark corner right at the back. The talk flowed this way and that. Then one of them raised the question of what each man thought he would wish for if he had a wish to spare. One wanted gold, another a son-in-law, a third a new carpenter's bench, and so it went the rounds. When each had said his piece, that still left the beggar in the dark corner. Reluctantly, after some hesitation, he gave in to his questioners: 'I'd wish I was a great and powerful king and ruled a large country and was lying asleep one night, in bed in my palace, when the enemy breached the frontier and horsemen reached the square in front of my palace before dawn and there was no resistance and I, starting up out of sleep, no time even to get dressed, wearing just my shirt, had to take flight and was chased up hill and down dale, through forests and mountains, day and night without let-up, until I had reached this bench in your corner, safe. That is what I wish.' The others looked at one another in bewilderment. 'But what would such a wish leave you with?' asked one. 'A shirt,' was the reply.

The story takes us deep into the economy of Kafka's world. Look, no one says that the distortions to correct which the Messiah will one day appear are only distortions of our space. They are also, surely, distortions of our time. Kafka certainly thought so. And out of that certainty had his grandfather say, ' "Life is astonishingly short. As I look back on it now it becomes so telescoped in my mind that I have difficulty in understanding how a young man can come to a decision to ride to the next village without being afraid that – leaving possible misfortunes quite out of account – even the span of a normal, fortune-favoured existence will be wholly inadequate for the trip."' A brother to that old man is the beggar who, in his 'normal, fortune-favoured existence', fails even to find time for a wish, but in the abnormal existence, ill-favoured by fortune, of the flight on which he sets out with his story is above that wish and swaps it for its fulfilment.

But there is amongst Kafka's creations a clan who do, in their peculiar way, reckon with the shortness of life. They come from that 'city in the south, of which [it used to be said]: "There are people for you! Just think – they never go to sleep!" "And why don't they?" "Because they don't get tired." "And why don't they?" "Because they're fools." "Don't fools get tired, then?" "How could fools get tired?"' Clearly, these fools are related to the assistants, who also never get tired. However, with this clan things go beyond that. We find casual mention of the fact that the assistants' faces '"[. . .] suggest adults, even perhaps students"'. And indeed students, who in Kafka crop up in the strangest places, are the spokespersons and rulers of this lineage. '"But when do you sleep?" Karl asked, looking at the student in amazement. "Seriously – sleep?" said the student. "I'll sleep when I've finished my studies."' One cannot help thinking of children: the reluctance with which they go off to bed! After all, something might happen when they are asleep that makes some call upon them. 'Don't forget the best!' the comment goes, a comment that is 'familiar to us from an untold wealth of ancient stories, despite its possibly not occurring in any of them'. But forgetting always concerns the best because it concerns the possibility of release/redemption. ' "The idea of wishing to help me," the restlessly wandering spirit of Gracchus the hunter says ironically, "is an illness and must be cured in bed." ' While studying, the students stay awake, and it may be the highest virtue of their studies to keep them awake. The fasting-artist fasts, the doorkeeper says nothing, and the students stay awake. It is in such concealment that, in Kafka, the great rules of asceticism operate.

Studying is their crown. Reverently Kafka brings that crown to light out of those buried boyhood days. 'Not so very differently (it was a long time ago now), Karl had sat at table in the parental home, doing his homework, while his father read the paper or made entries in the ledgers and dealt with correspondence for a society and his mother busied herself with some needlework, tugging the thread high in the air above the material. In order not to get in his father's way, Karl had put only the exercise book and writing implements on the table and arranged the books he needed on chairs to right and left. How quiet it had been there! And how seldom strangers had come into the room!'

Maybe such studies were nothing. Yet they are very close to the kind of nothing that alone makes the something useful – namely, the *Tao*. It was the *Tao* Kafka had in mind with his desire 'to hammer a table together with meticulously correct craftsmanship and at the same time do nothing, but not in a way that enabled people to say, "Hammering is nothing to him", making them say instead, "For him hammering is proper hammering and at the same time also a nothing," as a result of which the hammering would in fact have become even bolder, even more determined, even more real, and if you like even madder.' And the gesture executed by students studying is just as determined, just as fanatical. It cannot be thought of as more special. The clerks, the students are out of breath. They go dashing about. '"Often the official dictates so quietly that the writer cannot hear at all sitting down, he has to keep jumping up to catch the words, sitting down quickly to write, then jumping up again, and so on. The whole thing is so peculiar! It's almost incomprehensible."' But it may become more comprehensible when one thinks back to the actors of the Nature Theatre. Actors must respond to their cue with the speed of lightning. And there is another way in which they resemble the assiduous scribes. For them it really is true that '"hammering is proper hammering and at the same time also a nothing"' – namely, when it is in their part. They study that part; it would be a poor actor who forgot a word or a gesture from it. For the members of the Oklahoma troupe, however, it is their former life. Hence the 'nature' in this Nature Theatre. Its actors are released/redeemed. Not so the student whom Karl watches in silence from the balcony one night as he sits reading his book: '[he] turned the pages, now and then looked something up in another book, which he invariably reached for very quickly, and occasionally made notes in an exercise book, each time lowering his face surprisingly deeply towards the pages'.

Kafka is tireless in recalling gesture in this way. Yet this is never done otherwise than with astonishment. K. has justly been likened to Schweyk; one of them finds everything surprising, the other nothing. In an age of enormously increased alienation amongst people and of the unpredictably mediated relations that were now all they had to connect them to one another, film and the gramophone were invented. In film, a person fails to recognize his own walk, in the gramophone his own voice. Experiments prove this. The situation occupied by the subject in such experiments is Kafka's own situation. It is what points him in the direction of studying. Maybe in the process he will come across fragments of his own existence that still connect with his part. He would come to grasp the lost gesture as Peter Schlemihl did the shadow he had sold. He would understand himself, but at what monstrous effort! The fact is, what blows here from the direction of oblivion is a storm. And study is a ride that proceeds against it. The beggar on the bench round the stove rides in the direction of his past to apprehend himself in the figure of the fleeing king. On the one hand there is life, which is too short for a ride; on the other, this ride that is long enough for life '[. . .] till one stopped using the spurs, there being no spurs, till one threw away the reins, there being no reins, and one scarcely saw the terrain out in front as a well-mown stretch of moorland without even a horse's neck now or a horse's head'. In this way the imagination of the blissful rider finds fulfilment, the rider who races towards the past on an empty, merry journey, no longer a burden to his mount. But wretched the rider who is chained to his nag, having set his future destination in advance – even if it is the nearest: the coal-cellar. Wretched, too, his animal, both are wretched: the bucket and the rider. 'As bucket-rider, one hand high on the handle, the plainest bridle, I turn and laboriously descend the stairs; at the bottom, however, my bucket climbs, splendidly, splendidly; when camels, resting on the ground, rise to their feet, shaking themselves beneath the driver's staff, they look no lovelier.' No more hopeless prospect is offered by any region than by 'the regions of the Icy Mountains' into which the bucket-rider vanishes, never to be seen again. Out of 'the nethermost regions of death' blasts the wind that favours him – the same wind as in Kafka blows so often from the primeval world, the one by which the barque of Gracchus the hunter is also pushed along. 'Everywhere,' says Plutarch, 'in connection with mysteries and sacrifices, among both Greeks and barbarians, it is taught [. . .] there must be two distinct elemental beings and mutually opposing forces, one following the right-hand rule and pointing straight ahead while the other turns around and pushes backwards.' Turning around is the direction of studying, which transforms existence into scripture. Its chief instructor is Bucephalus, the 'New Attorney' who without the mighty Alexander (meaning: rid of the relentlessly advancing conqueror) takes the way back. 'Free, his flanks unburdened by the rider's loins, in quiet lamplight far from the din of Alexander's battles, he reads and turns the pages of our ancient codices.'

Some time ago this story was made the object of an exegisis by Werner Kraft. After carefully examining every detail of the text, the interpreter remarks: 'Nowhere in literature is there so monumental, so conclusive a critique of the whole body of myth as here.' The word 'justice', Kraft opines, is not one Kafka uses; nevertheless it is on justice that this critique of myth takes its stand. However, having come so far we risk missing Kafka if we stop here. Is it really law that could thus, in the name of justice, be invoked against myth? No, as a legal scholar Bucephalus remains true to his origins. He only appears (this might be what Kafka sees as new for Bucephalus and for the legal profession) not to practise. Law that is no longer practised but only studied is the gateway to justice.

The gateway to justice is study. Yet Kafka does not dare attach to such study the promises that tradition has linked to study of the Torah. His assistants are sidesmen who have mislaid their synagogue, his students pupils who have mislaid their scripture. Now nothing holds them back on the 'empty, merry journey'. Kafka, however, located the law of his own; once, at least, when he contrived to bring its breathtaking speed into line with the kind of epic march step he undoubtedly spent his whole life looking for. He committed it to a piece of writing, his most perfect piece of writing not only because it is an exegesis.

'Sancho Panza, who incidentally never boasted of the fact, managed over the years, by providing a quantity of courtly romances and tales of bandit life in the evening and night-time hours, to divert the attention of his devil (whom he later named Don Quixote) to such effect that the latter then groundlessly performed the craziest deeds, but in the absence of a predestined object, which should in fact have been Sancho Panza, these harmed no one. Sancho Panza, a free man, calmly followed Don Quixote on his toings and froings, possibly out of a certain sense of responsibility, and derived therefrom huge and useful entertainment until the end of his days.'

Staid fool and clumsy assistant, Sancho Panza sent his rider on ahead. Bucephalus had outlived his. Whether man or horse no longer matters so much, provided only that the burden has been removed from the back.

Picturing Proust

I

The thirteen volumes of Marcel Proust's *A la recherche du temps perdu* are the product of a unique synthesis in which the contemplation of the mystic, the art of the prose writer, the verve of the satirist, the knowledge of the scholar, and the self-absorption of the monomaniac all come together in an autobiographical work. It has rightly been said that all great works of literature either establish a genre or wind one up – in other words, are special cases. However, this is one of the hardest of them to pin down. Everything from structure (work of literature, book of memoirs, comment, all in *one*) to the syntax of endless sentences (the Nile of language here bursting its banks to fertilize the plains of truth) is outside the norm. That this great one-off of literature at the same time represents its greatest achievement in recent decades is the first revealing discovery confronting the reader. And in the highest degree unhealthy are the conditions underlying it. An out-of-the-ordinary illness, exceptional wealth and abnormal tendencies. Not everything about this life sets an example, yet it is all exemplary. It places the towering literary achievement of our age at the heart of impossibility, at the centre of (albeit simultaneously at the point of indifference to) all risks, and characterizes this great realization of a 'life's work' as the last for a long time. Proust's image is the highest physiological expression that the constantly growing discrepancy between poetry and life has managed to attain. That is the moral justification for this attempt to summon it up.

We know that Proust did not, in his work, describe a life as it had been but a life as the person who had lived it remembered that life. Yet even that is obscure and put far too coarsely. Because here, so far as the reminiscing author is concerned, the chief role is played not by what he experienced but by the weaving together of his memories, Penelope's labour of bearing things in mind. Or should we perhaps talk instead of Penelope's labour of forgetting? For surely involuntary bearing in mind, Proust's *mémoire involuntaire*, is much closer to forgetting than to what is usually referred to as memory? And surely this labour of spontaneously bearing things in mind, in which remembering is the weft and forgetting the warp, is actually the opposite of Penelope's labour, not its likeness. For this is where day undoes what night had brought about. Waking up each morning we hold in our hands, usually feebly and slackly, only frayed scraps of the tapestry of lived existence, as forgetting has woven it within us. Yet each day, with its purposive actions and even more with its purpose-rooted recall, unpicks the web, the ornamentation of forgetting. That is why towards the end of his life Proust turned day into night – he wished, in a darkened room, lit by artificial light, to devote his every hour, without interruption, to his work, determined not to miss a single one of those intertwined arabesques.

If the Romans called a text woven, there is scarcely one more woven and more densely so than Marcel Proust's. Nothing was dense enough for him and sufficiently enduring. According to his publisher, Gallimard, the way Proust corrected proofs was the despair of the typesetter. The galleys invariably came back filled right up to the edge with handwriting. Yet not a single printing error had been eliminated; all the available space was packed with fresh text. The laws of remembering affected the very scale of the work. The reason was that, while an event experienced is finally closed, at least in the one sphere of experience, an event remembered is limitless, being simply a key to all that came before and all that came after it. And there is another sense in which it is remembering that dictates the strict weaving pattern here. The fact is, the unity of the text stems solely from the *actus purus* of remembering. Not from the person of the author and certainly not from the plot. Indeed, the vagaries of the latter can be said to be merely the reverse side of the continuum of remembering, the pattern on the back of the tapestry. That was what Proust wanted, what he meant when he said he would really like to see his entire work printed in a single volume, with two columns to the page and no paragraph divisions at all.

What was he looking for so frantically? What lay behind all this tireless effort? Can we say that all life, all works, all deeds that count were never anything but the unswerving development of the most banal, most fleeting, most sentimental, feeblest hours in the existence of the person to whom they belong? And when Proust, in a famous passage, described these most personal hours of his, he did so in such a way that everyone rediscovers them in his or her own existence. We are a hair's breadth from being able to term that existence everyday. It comes with the night, with a lost chirruping, or with that deep breath taken while leaning out of a window. And there is no telling what encounters might have been meant for us had we worried less about sleeping. Proust paid no heed to sleep. And yet (or rather because of that) Jean Cocteau was able in a fine essay to say of Proust's tone of voice that it obeyed the laws of night and honey. By submitting to their dominion he overcame the hopeless grief inside him (what he once called *'l'imperfection incurable dans l'essence même du présent'* ['the incurable imperfection in the very essence of the present']) and built a house for his swarming thoughts from the honeycomb of remembering. Cocteau saw what ought to preoccupy every Proust reader in the highest degree: he saw the blind, absurd, obsessive demand for bliss in the man. It flashed from his every glance. His glances were not themselves blessed. But in them sat happiness/good fortune [the German word *Glück*, of uncertain etymology, carries both areas of meaning] as *in* gambling or *in* love. Nor is it hard to say why this heart-stopping, explosive will to bliss that permeates Proust's writing so seldom reaches his readers. Proust himself made it easier for them at many points to consider this *oeuvre* too from the tried-and-tested, comfortable viewpoint of renunciation, heroism, asceticism. What could make more sense to model students of life than that great achievement should be the fruit of nothing but toil, misery and disappointment? That such a thing as blessedness might also have a part in the beautiful would be too much for them; their resentment would never accept it.

However, there is a twofold will to bliss, a dialectics of the phenomenon. A hymnic and an elegiac form. One is the unheard-of, the unprecedented, the acme of good fortune. The other is the everlasting yet-again, the constantly repeated restoration of the original, primal state of bliss. It is this elegiac idea of bliss (we might also call it Eleatic) that for Proust transforms existence into a forest reserve of remembering. To it he sacrificed not only (in life) friends and society, but also (in his work) plot, unity of person, narrative flow, play of imagination. It was not the worst of his readers (Max Unold) who picked up the resultant 'boredom' of his writings in order to compare it with shaggy-dog stories, inventing the formula: 'He [Proust] has contrived to make the shaggy-dog story interesting. He says, "Just imagine, dear reader, yesterday I dunk a madeleine in my tea and it occurs to me that I was a child in the country . . ." – and he goes on for the next eighty pages, and the story is so riveting that one believes one is no longer the listener but the actual person day-dreaming.' In such yarns ('all normal dreams become "shaggy-dog stories" as soon as they are narrated'), Unold discovered the bridge to dream. Every synthetic interpretation of Proust must follow him. Plenty of invisible gateways lead in that direction. There is Proust's frantic studying, his enthusiastic cult of similarity. It is not in the places where he unexpectedly comes across it in works, in physiognomies, in turns of phrase, invariably to his alarm, that it allows the true signs of its dominion to be identified. The similarity of one entity with another that we take for granted, that preoccupies our waking hours, merely laps around the deeper dream world in which what occurs is never identical yet appears similar – inscrutably similar, even to itself. Children are aware of a symbol of this world, the sock, which has the structure of the dream world when, rolled up in the clothes drawer, it is simultaneously 'bag' and 'things brought along'. And as they can never get enough of turning both (bag and baggage) into something else (the sock) at *one* stroke, so Proust was insatiable when it came to emptying the dummy, the self, at a stroke in order to bring in, over and over again, that other thing, the image that fed his inquisitiveness – nay, his homesickness. He lay in bed ravaged by homesickness, homesickness for a world distorted in a state of similarity, the world in which the true surrealist face of existence breaks through. To it belongs what occurs in connection with Proust, no matter how discreetly and nobly it appears. To wit, never in isolation, dramatically and in a visionary manner, but heralded and often with backing, bearing a fragile, precious reality: the image. It detaches itself from the fabric of Proust's sentences in the same way as, in Balbec, under Françoise's hands, the summer's day emerges immemorially ancient, mummy-like, from the net curtains.

II

The most important thing a person has to say he will not invariably proclaim out loud. Nor, even quietly, will he always confide it to his confidant, the person closest to him, the one who most devotedly stands ready to take his confession. If it is not people alone but also ages that have this shy, actually crafty and rather frivolous way of conveying deeply private matters to just anyone, for the nineteenth century it is not Zola or Anatole France but the young Proust, the insignificant snob, the fantastical society man, who from the ageing era (as from that other person, the equally moribund Swann) caught the most astonishing secrets on the wing. It was Proust who made the nineteenth century a fit subject for memoirs. What before him was a lacklustre century became a force field in which a wide variety of currents were uncovered by later authors. Nor is it any accident that the most interesting work of this kind was written by someone, a woman, who knew Proust personally as an admirer and friend. The very title under which Princess Clermont-Tonnerre brought out the first volume of her memoirs (*Au temps des équipages*) would scarcely have been thinkable before Proust. Moreover, it conjures up a faint echo of the ambiguous, affectionate, challenging call issued by the writer from the Faubourg Saint-Germain. In addition, this (melodic) portrayal is full of direct or indirect links to Proust in its stance and in its characters, who include Proust himself and some of his favourite objects of study from the Ritz.

This puts us, of course (the fact cannot be denied) in an extremely feudal milieu, and with such phenomena as Robert de Montesquiou (of whom Princess Clermont-Tonnerre gives a splendid portrayal) in a very particular one at that. But so does Proust; moreover, as everyone knows, here too there is no lack of a Montesquiou equivalent. None of this would be worth discussing (especially since the question of the model is of secondary and so far as Germany is concerned of no importance) were it not for the fact that German criticism is so very fond of taking the easy way out. Above all, it was unable to let slip an opportunity to go slumming with the lending-library mob. So its hired experts were very ready to read back from the work's snobbish setting to the man who had penned these pages and to dismiss Proust's work as an internal French affair, a diverting supplement to the *Almanach de Gotha*. Yet it is obvious: the problems of Proust's people stem from a complacent society. But not one of those problems coincides with Proust's own. These are subversive. If one had to reduce them to a formula, his concern would be to construct the whole edifice of high society in the form of a physiognomy of tittle-tattle. There is nothing in the arsenal of its prejudices and maxims that his scathing comedy does not annihilate. Having been the first to point this out is not the least of the important services furnished by Léon Pierre-Quint as Proust's first interpreter. 'If the talk turns to humorous works,' Pierre-Quint writes, 'we usually think of short, funny books between illustrated covers. We forget *Don Quixote*, *Pantagruel* and *Gil Blas*, sprawling tomes in tiny print.' In this company, the subversive side of Proust's work comes out most conclusively. And here it is not so much humour as comedy that constitutes the core of his strength; he does not hold the world up to ridicule, he hurls it down to ridicule. At the risk of its smashing to pieces, whereupon he alone will shed tears. And it does smash to pieces, or rather its contents do: the unity of the family and the personality, sexual morality, respect for rank. The pretensions of the bourgeoisie explode amid ridicule. Their headlong retreat and their reassimilation by the aristocracy is the sociological subject of the work.

Proust never tired of the training required to move in feudal circles. Unflaggingly and without having to force himself much, he so fashioned his nature as to make it as unfathomable, inventive, obsequious and difficult as for the sake of his task he needed to become. Later, mystification and elaboration came so naturally to him that his letters are sometimes whole systems of parentheses (and not just grammatical ones, either). Letters that despite their endlessly witty and nimble composition occasionally recall that legendary device: 'Esteemed madam, I have this moment realized that I left my cane at your house yesterday. Would you please give it to the bearer of this letter? P.S.: I am so sorry to disturb you, I have just found it.' And how resourceful he is in difficulties. Late one night he appears at Princess Clermont-Tonnerre's residence, agreeing to stay on condition that the doctor is called out to attend him. He then proceeds to dispatch the valet, giving him a detailed description of the district and of the house, ending with: 'You can't miss it. The only window along Boulevard Haussmann where the light is still on.' Everything but the number. Try locating the address of a brothel in a foreign city, even if you have been given the most prolix instructions telling you everything except the name of the street and the number of the house, and you will understand what is meant here (and how it has to do with Proust's love of ceremony, his admiration for Saint-Simon, and last but not least his intransigent Frenchness). The quintessence of experience, surely, is learning how very difficult it is to find out many things that can in fact (ostensibly) be communicated in a few words. The trouble is, those words belong to a special jargon based on caste and social rank and incomprehensible to outsiders. No wonder the secret language of the salons so roused Proust's passion. When he later came to give a merciless description of the little Courvoisier clique, the *'esprit d'Oriane'*, he had himself, through frequenting the Bibescos, got to know the improvisations of a coded language to which we too have meanwhile been introduced.

In the years of his salon existence Proust developed not only the vice of flattery to an eminent (one might almost say 'theological') degree; he also developed that of inquisitiveness. On his lips was a reflection of the smile that, in the intrados of some of the cathedrals he so loved, flits like a brush fire over the lips of the foolish virgins. It is the smile of inquisitiveness. Was it inquisitiveness that basically made him such a great parodist? We should then, at the same time, know what we should think of the word 'parodist' as used here. Not a lot. For even if it does justice to his boundless malice it completely misses the bitter, savage, intractable nature of the splendid pieces of reportage that he wrote in the style of Balzac, Flaubert, Sainte-Beuve, Henri de Régnier, the Goncourts, Michelet, Renan and finally his darling Saint-Simon and that he collected in book form in *Pastiches et mélanges*. It is the mimicry of the inquisitive observer that constitutes the brilliant trick of this series – at the same time as it constitutes an element of Proust's entire output, in which a passion for the [physiologically] vegetable can never be taken seriously enough. Ortega y Gasset was the first to draw attention to the vegetative existence of Proust's characters, who are tied in so permanent a fashion to the place where they are found in society, determined by the standing of the feudal Sun of Grace, swayed by the wind that blows from Guermantes or Méséglise, impenetrably intertwined in the thicket of their fate. It is a life that gives rise to mimicry as literary method. Its most sharply focused, most obvious findings squat on their objects as insects sit on leaves, flowers and twigs, giving away nothing of their existence until a leap, a wing-beat, a start by the frightened observer indicates that here an unpredictable, entirely separate life has slipped inconspicuously into a foreign world. 'Metaphor,' says Pierre-Quint, 'no matter how unexpected, moulds itself closely to ideas.'

The true reader of Proust is repeatedly shaken by tiny frights. Moreover, he finds in metaphysics the expression of the same mimicry as must have struck him as the fight for existence of this spirit high up in the canopy of society. A word about how closely and fruitfully these two vices, inquisitiveness and flattery, were intertwined. A revealing passage in Princess Clermont-Tonnerre reads: 'And finally it has to be said that Proust would get quite carried away, studying the servants. Was it because an element he encountered nowhere else stimulated his intuition here, or did he envy them their being in a better position to observe intimate details of matters that tickled his fancy? Be that as it may – the domestic staff in all their various characters and types constituted his passion.' In the exotic hues of a Jupien, a Monsieur Aimé or a Céleste Albaret the line extends from a figure such as Françoise, who with the strong, sharp features of St Martha appears to have stepped bodily from the pages of a Book of Hours, all the way to those grooms and footmen who seem to be paid not for working but for doing nothing. And it may be that nowhere are the requirements of display of more eager interest to this connoisseur of ceremony than at these lowest ranks. Who is to say how much inquisitiveness about servants went into Proust's flattery, how much flattery of servants went into his inquisitiveness, and how far it went, this crafty copy of the servant role amid the upper reaches of social life? He made it, and he could not help doing so. Because as he reveals himself: *'voir'* and *'désirer imiter'* ['seeing' and 'wishing to emulate'] were one and the same so far as he was concerned. It was an attitude that, in all its superiority and servility, Maurice Barrès captured in one of the most distinctive things ever said about Proust: *'Un poète persan dans un loge concierge.'*

There was an element of the detective in Proust's inquisitiveness. To him, the top ten thousand were a criminal family, a bunch of conspirators like no other: the Camorra of consumers. It excludes from its world anyone who plays a part in production. Or demands that with grace and modesty they at least conceal that part behind the sort of air that consummate professionals of consumption affect. Proust's analysis of snobbery, which is of far greater importance than his apotheosis of art, attains its high point in his social criticism. For the attitude of the snob is nothing more nor less than the consistent, organized, hardened view of existence from the chemically pure standpoint of the consumer. And since the remotest as well as the most primitive memory of the productive forces of nature was banished from this satanic fairyland, even in love the inverted attachment suited Proust better than the normal. But the pure consumer is the pure exploiter. He is so logically and theoretically; in Proust he is so in all the concreteness of his current historical existence. Concrete because inscrutable and not to be placed. Proust portrays a class that is obliged in its entirety to disguise its material foundation and for that very reason is assigned to a feudalism that, having no economic importance in itself, lends itself all the more to being used as a mask for the *haute bourgeoisie*. This illusionless, ruthless breaker of the spell of self, of love and of morality (as Proust liked to see himself) makes of his entire, boundless art a veil concealing this one, vitally important mystery of his class: the economic. Not as if he were thereby being of service to it. He is simply ahead of it. What it lives begins, in him, to become comprehensible. Yet much of the greatness of this work will remain inaccessible or undiscovered until that class reveals its sharpest features in the final struggle.

III

In the last [nineteenth] century there used to be (I don't know if it is still there) a pub in Grenoble called *Au Temps perdu*. With Proust too we are guests, passing beneath a swinging sign and stepping over a threshold beyond which eternity and intoxication await us. Fernandez was right to distinguish in Proust a *thème de l'éternité* from the *thème du temps*. However, far from being Platonic and utopian, that eternity is intoxicating. So if 'time, for all who study its passage, exposes a new and hitherto unknown kind of eternity', this does not at all mean that the individual is thereby approaching 'the higher climes that a Plato or Spinoza reached with one beat of their wings'. No – because the fact is, there are in Proust rudiments of a surviving idealism. Yet it is not they that determine the importance of this work. The eternity in which Proust opens up aspects is enclosed time, not unbounded time. His true interest is in the passage of time in its most real nature – but that is a bounded nature and prevails nowhere in less distorted form than in remembering (internally) and in growing old (externally). Tracing the action and counteraction of ageing and remembering means penetrating to the heart of Proust's world, the universe of finitude. It is the world in a state of similarity, ruled by the *'correspondances'* that first Romanticism and then, most intimately, Baudelaire registered but that Proust (alone) contrived to bring out in our own lived lives. That is the work of *mémoire involontaire*, the rejuvenating force that is a match for the relentless ageing process. Where things past are reflected in the freshly dew-drenched 'now', a painful shock of rejuvenation once again inexorably gathers them up in the manner that, for Proust, the Guermantes way and Swann's way cross when (in volume thirteen) he wanders through the Combray district one last time and discovers how the paths intertwine. In no time the landscape veers round like a wind. *'Ah! que le monde est grand à la clarté des lampes! / Aux yeux du souvenir que le monde est petit!'* Proust's immense achievement has been in no time to cause the whole world to age by an entire human life. But that very concentration in which what normally just wilts and fades is suddenly, in a flash, burned up – that is called rejuvenation. *A la recherche du temps perdu* is a sustained attempt to load a whole existence with the highest possible degree of presence of mind. Proust proceeds not by reflection but by recall. He is positively permeated by the truth that we all of us lack the time to live the real dramas of the existence assigned to us. That makes us age. Nothing else. The lines and wrinkles in our faces are the entries recording the great passions, the vices, the discoveries that presented themselves at our door – but we, the people of the house, were not at home.

Scarcely has Western literature seen a more radical experiment in self-absorption since Loyola's *Spiritual Exercises*. This one too has at its centre a solitariness that with the power of the maelstrom drags the world down into its whirling. And the over-loud and inconceivably vacuous tittle-tattle that comes booming in our direction from the pages of Proust's novels is the roar with which society is plunging into the abyss of that solitariness.

This is where Proust's inveighing against friendship has its place. The silence at the bottom of this crater (its eyes are the most silent, sucking everything up) wished to be preserved. What, annoyingly and capriciously, emerges from so many anecdotes is the combination of an un-paralleled intensity of conversation with the most extreme remoteness from the interlocutor. Never before was anyone able to show us things as he did. His pointing finger is without equal. Yet there is another gesture in that most friendly of exchanges that is conversation: touch. The touch gesture is wholly foreign to Proust. He is incapable of touching his readers, either – quite incapable. Were literature to be arranged around these two poles (the pointing and the touching), Proust's work would constitute the centre of one pole, Péguy's of the other. This, basically, is what Fernandez understood so well: 'Depth or should one say penetration is always on his side, never on that of his partner.' With a dash of cynicism and great virtuosity, this comes out in his literary criticism. Its chief document is an essay written at the zenith of his fame and the nadir of his deathbed: '*A propos de Baudelaire*'. Jesuitical in acceptance of his own condition, excessive in the volubility of the man keeping to his bed, frightening in the indifference of the man doomed to die, who wants to say something more at this point, never mind what about. The thing that inspired him here, as he faced death, also determines his dealings with contemporaries: so jerky and harsh an alternation of sarcasm and affection, affection and sar-casm, that his subject threatens to collapse in exhaustion under it.

The man's provocative, restless side still affects the reader of the works. One need only think of the seemingly endless strings of '*soit que*' clauses that describe an action in an exhaustive, depressing fashion in the light of the countless motives that may have underlain it. Nevertheless, these paratactic perspectives show how in Proust weakness and genius are but one: the intellectual renunciation, the tried-and-tested scepticism that he brought to things. He came after the smug inwardnesses of Romanticism and was determined, as Jacques Rivière puts it, not to place the slightest credence in 'internal sirens'. Rivière continues: 'Proust approached life without the least interest in metaphysics, without the least constructivist tendency, without the least inclination to spread consolation.' Nothing is more true. Accordingly, then, even the work's basic shape, on the methodical nature of which Proust never tired of insisting, is not remotely a construction. Yet methodical it is in the sense that the lines on a hand are methodical or the arrangement of stamens in the calyx. Proust, the child-man, deeply weary, had slumped back on the bosom of nature, not in order to suck at its breast but in order, hearing its heartbeat, to dream. We must picture him as weak as that if we would understand how happy Jacques Rivière was to understand him out of weakness and be able to say, 'Marcel Proust died of the same inexperience as enabled him to write his work. He died of unworldliness and because he lacked the understanding to alter living conditions that had begun to crush him. He died because he did not know how to light a fire or how to open a window.' And of his nervous asthma, of course.

The doctors were powerless against this affliction. Not so the writer, who very methodically harnessed it in his service. He was (to start with the most external element) a perfect director of his illness. For months he associates with crushing irony the image of an admirer who sent him flowers with a fragrance he could not bear. And through the times and tides of his affliction he caused alarm to his friends, who dreaded and desired his sudden appearance, long after midnight, in the drawing room to which they had come themselves – a man *'brisé de fatigue'* and making, so he said, only a five-minute call who then stayed on until dawn, too tired to get to his feet again, too tired even to stop talking. Even the letter-writer never runs out of ways of deriving the most out-of-the-way effects from his condition. 'The rattle of my breathing drowns out the sound of my pen and that of a bath being drawn in the floor below.' But that is not all. Nor is the fact that his illness kept him from fashionable society. His asthma entered into his art, if it was not his art that gave rise to it. His syntax rhythmically mimics, step by step, this suffocation anxiety of his. And his ironical, philosophical, didactical musings are so many sighs of relief when the nightmare of remembering falls from his heart.

But on a larger scale it was death that was ever-present to him, mostly when he was writing – the menacing, suffocating throes of death. In this guise death confronted Proust, long before his affliction assumed critical forms. But not as a hypochondriac's fancy – as a *'réalité nouvelle'*, that new reality in which reactions to people and things constitute the lineaments of ageing. A stylistics of physiology would lead into the heart of that creative endeavour. For instance, no one who is aware of the peculiar toughness with which memories are preserved in the sense of smell (not smells in memory, not at all!) will be able to dismiss Proust's sensitivity to smells as in any way random. Certainly, most of the memories we look for come to us as visual images. And even the things that float up freely from the *mémoire involuntaire* are largely isolated visual images – somewhat mysteriously present. But that is precisely why, in order consciously to commit ourselves to the innermost rhythm of this writing, we must move to a particular level (the deepest one) of involuntary memory, the level at which the elements of memory no longer operate individually, as images, but as non-pictorial, formless, indeterminately weighty factors, bringing us tidings of an entity in much the same way as the heaviness of his net tells the fisherman something of his catch. Smell – that is the sense of weight of the person who casts his net on the waters of *'le temps perdu'*.

And his sentences are the entire musculature of the intelligible body; they constitute the whole unutterable effort of hauling that catch in.

One other point: the intimacy of the symbiosis between that specific creative endeavour and that specific physical affliction comes out most clearly in the fact that never, in Proust, is there an irruption of that heroic 'nevertheless' with which otherwise creative people rebel against their suffering. Hence it may be said on the other hand that an involvement in the way of the world and in living as profound as Proust's must inevitably have led to an ordinary, indolent kind of satisfaction on any other basis than an affliction so deep and unrelieved. As things were, however, that affliction was destined to have a *furor* without wishes or regrets show it its place in the great artistic process. For the second time there arose a scaffolding structure like the one from atop which Michelangelo, head bent back, painted *The Creation* on the Sistine Chapel ceiling: the sickbed in which Marcel Proust devoted the numberless pages that in the air he covered with his handwriting to the creation of his microcosm.

THE STORY OF PENGUIN CLASSICS

Before 1946 ... 'Classics' are mainly the domain of academics and students; readable editions for everyone else are almost unheard of. This all changes when a little-known classicist, E. V. Rieu, presents Penguin founder Allen Lane with the translation of Homer's *Odyssey* that he has been working on in his spare time.

1946 Penguin Classics debuts with *The Odyssey*, which promptly sells three million copies. Suddenly, classics are no longer for the privileged few.

1950s Rieu, now series editor, turns to professional writers for the best modern, readable translations, including Dorothy L. Sayers's *Inferno* and Robert Graves's unexpurgated *Twelve Caesars*.

1960s The Classics are given the distinctive black covers that have remained a constant throughout the life of the series. Rieu retires in 1964, hailing the Penguin Classics list as 'the greatest educative force of the twentieth century.'

1970s A new generation of translators swells the Penguin Classics ranks, introducing readers of English to classics of world literature from more than twenty languages. The list grows to encompass more history, philosophy, science, religion and politics.

1980s The Penguin American Library launches with titles such as *Uncle Tom's Cabin*, and joins forces with Penguin Classics to provide the most comprehensive library of world literature available from any paperback publisher.

1990s The launch of Penguin Audiobooks brings the classics to a listening audience for the first time, and in 1999 the worldwide launch of the Penguin Classics website extends their reach to the global online community.

The 21st Century Penguin Classics are completely redesigned for the first time in nearly twenty years. This world-famous series now consists of more than 1300 titles, making the widest range of the best books ever written available to millions – and constantly redefining what makes a 'classic'.

The Odyssey continues ...

The best books ever written

PENGUIN CLASSICS

SINCE 1946

Find out more at www.penguinclassics.com